SELF DEVELOPMENT:

ESSAYS ON ISLAMIC SPIRITUALITY

Mohammad Ali Shomali

D1513778

SELF DEVELOPMENT:

ESSAYS ON ISLAMIC SPIRITUALITY

Mohammad Ali Shomali

ISBN: 978-1-904934-11-0

© Institute of Islamic Studies, 2016

First published in Great Britain in 2016

by

Institute of Islamic Studies,

Islamic Centre of England

140 Maida Vale, London W9 1QB

Tel: (44) 0207 604 5500; Fax: (44) 0207 604 4898

Email: icel@ic-el.com

Table of Contents

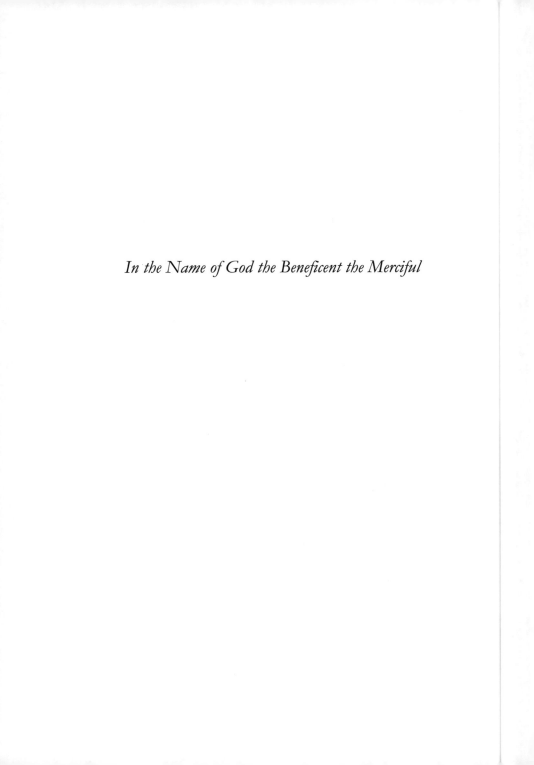

In the Name of God the Beneficent the Merciful

Introduction

Human beings differ from animals in many ways. One way is in their need and search for purpose and meaning in life. Whilst meeting basic needs can make animals very happy and satisfied, human beings look for something beyond this. They need something that can give them a good reason to go beyond daily routines and to face the constant challenges and struggles of life. Whilst any kind of war, conflict or confrontation in the world around us can very much disturb our life, it is only inner peace and tranquillity which can bring about a deep sense of contentment. This is why we witness that those who are better off and enjoy peace and security may have greater understanding of the need for a meaningful life and more clearly and strongly express their thirst for spirituality compared to many of those who experience difficulties in day to day life.

In Islam, spirituality occupies a very lofty and central position. According to the Qur'an and Islamic narrations, one of the main tasks of Prophet Muhammad (s) was to help people with "purification of their souls" and "accomplishment of noble traits of character." Life without a deep sense of meaning and purpose and void of devotion to God is "merely amusement and

6 SELF DEVELOPMENT

diversion and glitter and mutual vainglory among you and covetousness for wealth and children —like the rain whose vegetation impresses the farmer; then it withers and you see it turn yellow, then it becomes chaff...; and the life of this world is nothing but the wares of delusion (57:20)." Life filled with remembrance of God and movement towards Him brings peace to the heart, "*for without doubt in the remembrance of God do hearts find satisfaction. (13:28)*" Imam Sajjad (a) says:

> *Nothing will cool my burning thirst but reaching You, quench my ardour but meeting You, dampen my yearning but gazing upon Your face, settle my settling place without closeness to You.*[1]

The "Face of God" (*wajhullah*) has such an attraction for the human spirit that even a glimpse of it is enough to bring focus to a human being's life, to give a single orientation to all their undertakings [2] and to make them totally unable to go anywhere

---

[1] *The Psalms of Islam*, pp. 251 & 252.

[2] In Dua of Kumayl, Imam Ali (a) says:

يا رب يا رب يا رب أسألك بحقك و قدسك و أعظم صفاتك و أسمائك أن

تجعل أوقاتى من [فى] الليل و النهار بذكرك معمورة و بخدمتك موصولة و أعمالى

عندك مقبولة حتى يكون أعمالى و إرادتى [و أورادى] كلها وردا واحدا و حالى فى

خدمتك سرمدا

My Lord! My Lord! My Lord! I ask You by Your Right and Your Holiness and the greatest of Your Attributes and Names, that You makest my times in the night and the day inhabited by Your remembrance, and joined to Your service and my works acceptable to

else or to think of anything else;[1] rather with God's light upon them, a human being can go everywhere with God and do everything in a Godly manner. "Neither business nor trading would distract [them] from remembering God (24:37)."

In Munajat Sha'baniyyah, we read:

> *My God! Make me completely cut off from all else but You and enlighten the vision of our hearts with the radiance of looking at You until the vision of our hearts penetrates the veils of light and reaches the Source of Grandeur and set our spirit to be suspended at the glory of Your sanctity.[2]*

As I have said elsewhere, to be cut off from anything other than God means to be free from reliance on anything other than God and see everything as His sign and manifestation of His power and grace. The true servants of God, whether they are rich or poor, powerful or weak, famous or unknown, in ease or in adversity and whether they live alone or amongst people within society, are totally mindful of God and remember Him abundantly and therefore they have ultimate peace.

You, so that my works and my litanies may all be a single litany and my occupation with Your service everlasting.
[1] Imam Sajjad (a) says:

من ذا الذى ذاق حلاوة محبتک فرام منک بدلا

Oh My Lord! Who is the one who has tasted the sweetness of Your love and then has looked for a substitute."
[2] *Iqbal al-a'mal*, vol. 2, p. 687.

8 SELF DEVELOPMENT

Although experiencing such a deep sense of purpose in life and connection with God needs and involves practical action, knowledge always remains a key for it.

This book is a collection of eight papers on different aspects of Islamic spirituality. These papers are based on different lectures or workshops on this subject conducted in different contexts and on different continents. For example, in the academic year 2000-2001, I gave three lectures at e Ampleforth Abbey in North Yorkshire. The first lecture was an introduction to Islam. The second was on Islamic spirituality and the third was on some practical instructions given by Muslim mystics. In the same year, whilst I was finishing writing of *Shi'i Islam: Origin, Faith and Practices,* I decided to dedicate a chapter to rationality, spirituality and the search for justice as three major and general characteristics of Shi'a Islam. The framework that I have suggested and used over the years for organising ideas about Islamic spirituality was written at that time. Later I gave two lectures on spiritual direction in the second and third Catholic – Shi'a Dialogues in July 2005 at Ampleforth Abbey and in July 2007 at Worth Abbey. In April and May 2007, we had an eight session course on self-building at the Islamic Centre of England. On the 2nd June 2007, we had a one day seminar on self-purification at the Bayview Centre in Toronto. On the 11th June 2011, we had a one day programme on the systematic approach to spirituality at the Az-Zahra Islamic Centre in Vancouver.

Based on these lectures, especially the ones delivered in 2007 at the Islamic Centre of England, the first seven essays in this volume have been published in the *Message of Thaqalayn* in 2009 and 2010.

The last essay in this volume is on the theme of light in the Islamic world view in general and spirituality in particular. My serious reflections on this subject started during Hajj when I was giving talks on spirituality to the pilgrims in our group. In the academic year 2008-2009, I led a course on Islamic Spirituality at Jami'at al-Zahra for a group of PhD students. Then we were able to develop this notion further and based on my notes from that course, I gave a series of seven lectures at the Islamic Centre of England in July 2009 entitled, "Islamic Self Building, Advanced." These lectures are being published in the *Spiritual Quest* in a series entitled, "A Journey from Darkness to Light: the Qur'anic Perspective on the Concept of Light."

All the above lectures and papers were conducted or written in English. In 2010, whilst in the plane on my way to Washington D.C., I decided to write a summary of the discussion on light in Farsi and this is how most of the last essay in this volume was originally written. Something interesting happened that might be worth mentioning here. After arrival in D.C., whilst in the queue for immigration, I realized that I had left what I had written in the plane which was parked very far from the immigration hall and from which we had been brought by special buses. I felt a deep sense of loss in my heart but then caught sight of one of the staff of the same airline with which I had travelled and having explained the situation to them, alhamdulillah they then brought the papers back to me. So the time and energy spent on writing about "light" was not wasted [and perhaps never will be]. Later this paper was translated into English and was published in the *Message of Thaqalayn* in the Winter 2014 issue.

I take this opportunity to thank all the people who have been, in one way or another, involved in the above lectures, courses and publications. May Allah (swt) reward all who helped and contributed! Last, but by no means least, I feel obliged to express my deepest gratitude to Allah (swt) for what cannot be described in words. Without a doubt, if there has been any, even the slightest, success or goodness, it was because of His favour and guidance and when there have been shortcomings, they were due to me. If there is light, it comes from Him and if there is darkness, it is because we have not turned towards Him properly or, God forbid, we have turned away from Him.

May Allah (swt) bless all you who read this small book and take you nearer to Him, so much so that you would find Him closer to yourself than any intimate friend or loving relative!

Mohammad Ali Shomali

London, 30th November 2015

The Significance of Self-control and Self-purification[1]

It is a common idea amongst all religious and spiritual traditions that human beings should have some kind of self-control. Although we enjoy free will, we need to exercise our free will in a responsible way. In the same way that we expect others to respect our dignity and interests, we should respect dignity and interests of others. We should also safeguard our own dignity and long term interests. Thus, we cannot simply go after our whims and desires and do whatever we want. We need to have self-control and self-discipline which leads to self-purification. If we purify our hearts we will no longer need to resist our temptations and control ourselves against lower desires and lusts, since a purified person desires nothing except what is good and moral for himself and others. In what follows, we will study the necessity of self-control and self-purification.

Self-control

On the necessity of self-control, the Glorious Qur'an says:

---

[1] This essay is a revised version of a similar title published in the *Message of Thaqalayn*, vol. 10, no. 1.

وَ أَمَّا مَنْ خَافَ مَقَامَ رَبِّهِ وَ نَهَى النَّفْسَ عَنِ الْهَوَى فَإِنَّ الْجَنَّةَ هِيَ الْمَأْوَى

And as for him who fears to stand in the presence of his Lord and forbids his own soul from its whims and caprices then surely Paradise is the abode. (79:40 & 41)

يا دَاوُدُ ... لَا تَتَّبِعِ الْهَوَى فَيُضِلَّكَ عَنْ سَبِيلِ اللَّهِ إِنَّ الَّذِينَ يَضِلُّونَ عَنْ سَبِيلِ اللَّهِ لَهُمْ عَذَابٌ شَدِيدٌ بِما نَسُوا يَوْمَ الْحِسابِ

O David! ...do not follow the whims of your own soul for they will lead you astray from Allah's path. (38:26)

يا أَيُّهَا الَّذِينَ آمَنُوا كُونُوا قَوَّامِينَ بِالْقِسْطِ شُهَدَاءَ لِلَّهِ وَ لَوْ عَلَى أَنْفُسِكُمْ أَوِ الْوالِدَيْنِ وَ الْأَقْرَبِينَ إِنْ يَكُنْ غَنِيًّا أَوْ فَقِيراً فَاللَّهُ أَوْلَى بِهِما فَلا تَتَّبِعُوا الْهَوَى أَنْ تَعْدِلُوا وَ إِنْ تَلْوُوا أَوْ تُعْرِضُوا فَإِنَّ اللَّهَ كانَ بِما تَعْمَلُونَ خَبِيراً

O you who have faith! Be maintainers of justice and witnesses for the sake of Allah, even if it should be against yourselves or [your] parents and near relatives, and whether it be [someone] rich or poor, for Allah has a greater right over them. So do not follow [your] desires, lest you should be unfair, and if you distort [the testimony] or disregard [it], Allah is indeed well aware of what you do. (4:135)

Here we find two pieces of advice. Firstly, to observe Allah's Will, to fear Him and to try to obey Him. And secondly, to forbid our soul from doing what is wrong and harmful to us. This becomes only possible when we have some kind of self-control. In *Nahj al-Balaghah*, there is a very beautiful and insightful description of an un-named brother. Imam Ali (a) is quoted as saying:

كَانَ لِى فِيمَا مَضَى أَخٌ فِى اللَّهِ وَ كَانَ يُعَظِّمُهُ فِى عَيْنِى صِغَرُ الدُّنْيَا فِى
عَيْنِهِ ... وَكَانَ إِذَا بَدَهَهُ أَمْرَانِ يَنْظُرُ أَيُّهُمَا أَقْرَبُ إِلَى الْهَوَى فَيُخَالِفُهُ

*In the past I had a brother-in-faith, and he was prestigious
in my view because the world was insignificant in his eyes...
If two things confronted him he would see which was more
akin to his whims and he would do the other.*[1]

We see that one of the brother-in-faith's qualities was that when
faced with two options, (for example whether to go to one place
or another, one meeting or another or to engage in one business
or another), that is, when he was at a 'crossroads' and wanted to
choose which way to turn, he would look at his own soul/heart,
trying to discover which course of action was dearer to his self,
his own personal interest and then he would do the other one.
For example, one might have the option to either watch TV or to
help someone with his work. The soul which is not trained may
encourage us to go and watch TV, saying that it is a waste of time
to help the other person. But instead it is better to spend the time
helping the other person.

Of course, we may not always be able to find out what is the right
course of action by just following this instruction. But it is
important to at least try to find out what our selfish desire wants
us to do. Allah (swt) has given us the ability to distinguish
between what our egoism or greediness wants from us and those
things which are in our 'real' interests. When we work for our

---

[1]*Nahj al-Balaghah,* p. 526, Wise Sayings, no. 289

'real' interest we also secure the interests of other people. Allah (swt) has created us in a way that when we really serve ourselves, then we serve all human beings. But if we try to be 'clever' and only serve ourselves, then we not only damage ourselves but also others. There are lots of ways to damage ourselves and others. But it is not possible to truly serve oneself and not serve others.

There is also another method which we can use when we want to make a decision and have two or three options to consider and do not know what to do. In such cases, it is useful to try to imagine that a person who is very pious, and whose actions you trust and accept, is in your place. Then try to decide what that person would do if he were in your place. Since you have information about the way that person normally makes his decisions and about his intentions and good will, by keeping that person in mind you may be able to understand what to do. For example, you could imagine a pious scholar or pious relative, not necessarily an infallible or saint. You could then think about what they might do and this would give you some kind of insight.

So, it is a basic fact that we must have self-control. If we believe that we should just do what we want by satisfying and gratifying ourselves, then there is no point in talking about spiritual direction. Of course, Islam tells us that self-control is just a beginning; it is for those people who are at the start of the journey. What we need to do is to transform our soul from one which has an interest in lower desires into a soul which instead has a yearning for good things. Then our soul itself becomes a helper and an assistant to us. But this is a matter of training and purifying the soul.

There is a beautiful story in the *Mathnawi* by Rumi which shows how the heart can be transformed in either a good way or a bad way. Rumi says that once there was a perfume market where every person who wanted to sell perfumes had a shop. As a result, whoever entered this bazaar would only sense the beautiful fragrance of perfumes. Everyone enjoyed it, especially the perfume sellers who of course are the best people to appreciate perfume due to their refined sense of smell, whereas we become confused after smelling too many different fragrances. But one day someone went to the bazaar with a horse and the horse dirtied the passageway of the bazaar. The people became very angry because they could not tolerate the bad smell but no-one had the strength to take the dirt outside. It was like torture for them. So someone suggested that they had better bring someone there whose job was to clean horses' stables. They went to ask a young man to help them. He said that of course he would be able to do this as this was his job and what he always did. But when he entered the bazaar, before even reaching the dirty place, as soon as he smelt the fragrance of perfume he became unconscious because he was used to bad smells and so could not tolerate good fragrances.

In a similar way, on one hand, we find people who enjoy praying, who enjoy having some private time with Allah (swt). And, on the other hand, we find people who become angry when they see you praying and it causes them pain. And when they see you go to the mosque or the church, they feel troubled by this. There is a hadith which says that a believer in the mosque is like a fish in water but when a hypocrite is in the mosque he feels like he is in prison and always wants to escape. So these are the different states of the soul that we can reach through self-training and self-purification.

Self-purification

In the Glorious Qur'an, Allah (swt) emphasises the purification and purity of the human soul as follows:

وَ الشَّمْسِ وَ ضُحاها وَ الْقَمَرِ إِذا تَلاها وَ النَّهارِ إِذا جَلَّاها وَ اللَّيْلِ إِذا يَغْشاها وَ السَّماءِ وَ ما بَناها وَ الْأَرْضِ وَ ما طَحاها وَ نَفْسٍ وَ ما سَوَّاها فَأَلْهَمَها فُجُورَها وَ تَقْواها قَدْ أَفْلَحَ مَنْ زَكَّاها وَ قَدْ خابَ مَنْ دَسَّاها

I swear by the sun and its brilliance and the moon when it follows the sun and the day when it makes manifest the sun (and her beauty) and the night when it covers the sun and the heaven and Him who made it and the earth and Him who extended it and the soul and Him who made it perfect, then He inspired it to understand what is right and wrong for it. He will indeed be successful who purifies it and he will indeed fail whoever pollutes and corrupts it. (91:1-10)

So, after swearing eleven times, after so much emphasis, Allah (swt) declares that the person who purifies his soul will be successful and whoever pollutes and corrupts his soul will fail. On the Day of Judgement there will be two groups of people:

those who are prosperous and happy because they purified their soul and those who are in an unfortunate position because they were careless and negligent of their soul.

Purification of the soul is a prerequisite for closeness to Allah (swt). Indeed, the whole point of morality and spirituality is to purify one's soul. It is only then that the soul starts shining, receiving and reflecting utmost radiation and light from Allah (swt). If we want to meet Allah (swt), Who is the Most Pure, then we need to achieve purity. It is impossible to be polluted and then try to go towards Allah (swt). If we want to go somewhere where the people are smart, well-dressed and beautiful, then we too need to make ourselves clean and tidy, we should put on good clothes and thus make ourselves somehow compatible with them. Otherwise they will say that we will spoil their gathering and damage their reputation.

One of the main tasks of all the Prophets (a) and a major aim behind all their endeavours in teaching the divine message was to help people to purify their souls. Referring to the mission of Prophet Muhammad (s), the Glorious Qur'an says:

هُوَ الَّذى بَعَثَ فى الأُمِّيّنَ رَسُولاً مِنْهُمْ يَتْلُوا عَلَيْهِمْ آياتِهِ وَ يُزَكِّيهِمْ وَ يُعَلِّمُهُمُ الْكِتابَ وَ الْحِكْمَةَ وَ إِنْ كانُوا مِنْ قَبْلُ لَفى ضَلالٍ مُبينٍ

He is the one who has sent amongst illiterate people an apostle from among themselves who recites to them His verses and purifies them and teaches them the Book and the wisdom. (62:2)

لَقَدْ مَنَّ اللَّهُ عَلَى الْمُؤْمِنِينَ إِذْ بَعَثَ فِيهِمْ رَسُولاً مِنْ أَنْفُسِهِمْ يَتْلُوا عَلَيْهِمْ

آيَاتِهِ وَ يُزَكِّيهِمْ وَ يُعَلِّمُهُمُ الْكِتَابَ وَ الْحِكْمَةَ وَ إِنْ كَانُوا مِنْ قَبْلُ لَفِى

ضَلَالٍ مُبِينٍ

Certainly Allah conferred a great favour upon the believers when He raised among them a Messenger from among themselves, reciting to them His verses and purifying them, and teaching them the Book and the wisdom, although before that they were surely in manifest error. (3:164)

كَمَا أَرْسَلْنَا فِيكُمْ رَسُولاً مِنْكُمْ يَتْلُوا عَلَيْكُمْ آيَاتِنَا وَ يُزَكِّيكُمْ وَ يُعَلِّمُكُمُ

الْكِتَابَ وَ الْحِكْمَةَ وَ يُعَلِّمُكُمْ مَا لَمْ تَكُونُوا تَعْلَمُونَ

As We sent to you an Apostle from among yourselves, who recites to you Our signs, and purifies you, and teaches you the Book and wisdom, and teaches you what you did not know. (2:151)

Thus we see that one of the tasks of the Holy Prophet (s), in addition to reciting the Qur'an and teaching the Qur'an and wisdom, was to help us to purify our souls. Indeed, the appointment of Prophet Muhammad (s) for such tasks was an answer to the prayer of Abraham (a) and Ishmael (a) after they raised the foundations of the House (*ka'bah*):

وَ إِذْ يَرْفَعُ إِبْرَاهِيمُ الْقَوَاعِدَ مِنَ الْبَيْتِ وَ إِسْمَاعِيلُ رَبَّنَا تَقَبَّلْ مِنَّا إِنَّكَ

أَنْتَ السَّمِيعُ الْعَلِيمُ رَبَّنَا وَ اجْعَلْنَا مُسْلِمَيْنِ لَكَ وَ مِنْ ذُرِّيَّتِنَا أُمَّةً مُسْلِمَةً

لَكَ وَ أَرِنَا مَنَاسِكَنَا وَ تُبْ عَلَيْنَا إِنَّكَ أَنْتَ التَّوَّابُ الرَّحِيمُ رَبَّنَا وَ ابْعَثْ

فِيهِمْ رَسُولاً مِنْهُمْ يَتْلُوا عَلَيْهِمْ آيَاتِكَ وَ يُعَلِّمُهُمُ الْكِتَابَ وَ الْحِكْمَةَ وَ
يُزَكِّيهِمْ إِنَّكَ أَنْتَ الْعَزِيزُ الْحَكِيمُ

*Our Lord! Accept from us; surely You are the Hearing, the
Knowing….Our Lord! And raise up in them a Messenger
from among them who shall recite to them Your verses and
teach them the Book and the wisdom, and purify them;
surely You are the Mighty, the Wise.* (2:127-129)

Just imagine how wise Abraham was! How lovely his supplication
was! In three places in the Qur'an, Allah (swt) says that He has
sent the Holy Prophet (s) to do the same thing that Abraham (a)
and Ishmael (a) had wanted: to recite for the people the verses of
the divine Book, to teach them the divine Book and wisdom and
to purify their souls. Of course, it must be Allah (swt) Himself
who inspired them to pray in this way. Allah (swt) is so merciful
that He first invites us to call Him, then He inspires us what to
ask and then he answers our call and prayer.

Thus purification of the people was an important task for the
Holy Prophet (s) and, indeed, all the Prophets (a). These verses
clearly show the great significance of the task of purification of
the soul. It is noteworthy that in the prayer of Abraham (a) and
Ishmael (a) the request of teaching the Book and wisdom is
mentioned before the purification, but in all the three places that
Allah (swt) describes the mission of Prophet Muhammad (s),
purification precedes teaching the Book and wisdom. This
indicates the priority and great importance of purification. This

also suggests that a prerequisite for learning the Book and wisdom is to be pure.

There are a number of sources of impurity. A major or the major source of impurity is the attachment to the materialistic life and worldly affairs to the extent that Prophet Muhammad (s) said:

$$حُبُّ الدُّنْيَا رَأْسُ كُلِّ خَطِيئَةٍ أَلاتَرَى كَيْفَ أَحَبَّ مَا أَبْغَضَهُ اللَّهُ وَ أَيُّ خَطَإٍ أَشَدُّ جُرْماً مِنْ هَذَا$$

The attachment to this world is the source for every wrong. Beware how the one who is attached to this world has loved what Allah dislikes. What wrong can be a greater crime than this?[1]

The materialistic life (*dunya*) is the least important and valuable thing in the sight of Allah (swt). To be attached to it and make it one's ultimate end in one's life is a grave mistake and impurity. Therefore, one of the major treatments of this problem and a crucial means of purification of the soul is to ask people to give alms. In some twenty verses of the Qur'an, giving alms (*al-zakat*) is mentioned right after establishing prayer (*iqamat a-salat*). For example, Allah (swt) says in the Qur'an:

$$وَ ما أُمِرُوا إِلاَّ لِيَعْبُدُوا اللَّهَ مُخْلِصِينَ لَهُ الدِّينَ حُنَفاءَ وَ يُقِيمُوا الصَّلاةَ وَ يُؤْتُوا الزَّكاةَ وَ ذلِكَ دِينُ الْقَيِّمَةِ$$

---

[1] *Bihar al-Anwar*, vol. 67, p. 315.

And they were not commanded except to worship Allah, dedicating their faith to Him as men of pure faith, and to maintain the prayer, and pay the zakat. That is the upright religion. (98:5)

Zakat is derived from the same root as *tazkiyah* (purification) i.e. *za-ka-wa* which means growth and purity. It has been suggested1 that the reason for calling alms "zakat" lies in the fact that paying zakat purifies one's money and possessions. It is also true that paying alms causes growth (*namā*) and blessing (*barakah*) in one's money and sustenance. It seems more reasonable to suggest that the main reason for calling alms "*zakat*" is that it helps in purifying the soul by getting rid of the love for this world. This is why Allah (swt) says to Prophet Muhammad (s):

خُذْ مِنْ أَمْوَالِهِمْ صَدَقَةً تُطَهِّرُهُمْ وَ تُزَكِّيهِمْ بِهَا وَ صَلِّ عَلَيْهِمْ إِنَّ صَلَاتَكَ سَكَنٌ لَهُمْ وَ اللَّهُ سَمِيعٌ عَلِيمٌ

Take charity from their possessions to cleanse them and purify them thereby, and bless them. Indeed your blessing is a comfort to them, and Allah is all-hearing, all-knowing. (9:103)

In this verse, instead of the term *zakat*, *sadaqah* (charity) is used. However, the same point is there: Giving money for the sake of

---

1 *Lisan al-'Arab*, vol. 14, p. 358.

Allah (swt) helps in purification of the giver.1 Elsewhere the Qur'an says:

$$ اَلَّذِى يُؤْتِى مالَهُ يَتَزَكَّى وَ ما لِأَحَدٍ عِنْدَهُ مِنْ نِعْمَةٍ تُجْزَى إِلاَّ ابْتِغاءَ وَجْهِ $$

$$ رَبِّهِ الْأَعْلى وَ لَسَوْفَ يَرْضى $$

he who gives his wealth to purify himself and does not expect any reward from anyone, but seeks only the pleasure of his Lord, the Most Exalted, and, surely, soon he will be well-pleased. (92:18-21)

Thus when someone spends some money for the sake of Allah (swt) on things such as giving to the needy people or building places for common good such as Mosques, seminaries, schools and hospitals both giver and receiver benefit. However, the main beneficiary is the giver who is giving some money which is the least valuable thing in the sight of Allah (swt) and instead achieves purity and pleasure of Allah (swt).

$$ إِنَّما تُنْذِرُ الَّذينَ يَخْشَوْنَ رَبَّهُمْ بِالْغَيْبِ وَ أَقامُوا الصَّلاةَ وَ مَنْ تَزَكَّى فَإِنَّما $$

$$ يَتَزَكَّى لِنَفْسِهِ وَ إِلَى اللَّهِ الْمَصيرُ ... $$

You can only warn those who fear their Lord in secret, and maintain the prayer. Whoever seeks purification for himself, seeks purification only for his own sake, and to Allah is the return. (35:18)

---

[1] This in addition to the great emphasis that the Qur'an puts on giving alms shows that it is not just a linguistic point or an accident that paying zakat as a religious requirement and *tazkiyah* (purification of the people) as a major task of the Prophet (s) are so closely linked to each other.

Conclusion

It is a basic fact that we must have self-control. There can be no spirituality without self-discipline. We cannot develop ourselves by simply doing what we wish and satisfying and gratifying our soul. Of course, Islam tells us that self-control is just a beginning. What we need to do is to transform our soul from one which has an interest in lower desires into a soul which instead has a yearning for good things. By training and purifying our souls, our soul itself becomes a helper and an assistant to us. A major task of the Prophets and in particular Prophet Muhammad (s) was to help people to purify themselves. The reason for such a great emphasis on self-purification is the fact that Allah (swt) is the Most Pure and the Most Perfect and it is only by purification of the soul that we can achieve our ambition of getting close to Him. One major way of purification is to get rid of attachment to the materialistic life by giving out one's own money for the sake of Allah (swt).

Different Methodological Approaches to Spirituality[1]

In this essay we will review and briefly discuss different methodologies among Muslim scholars in studying spirituality in general and morality (*akhlaq*) in particular. In general, we can classify the attitudes of scholars into three main approaches:

1. The Philosophical Approach

2. The Mystical Approach

3. The Scriptural or Text-Based Approach

The Philosophical Approach

Many Muslim scholars have found the outlook of some Greek philosophers, especially Aristotle, to a large extent appealing as a way in which to speak about the human soul. According to this view, the human soul has three different faculties (*quwwah*) responsible for action; they are:

---

[1] This essay is a revised version of a similar title published in the *Message of Thaqalayn*, vol. 10, no. 2.

1. The rational faculty (*al-quwwah al-'aqliyyah*) is the faculty responsible for knowledge. It helps us to understand matters and enables us to engage in discussion. If this faculty functions properly, one can attain true wisdom (*hikmah*). This does not mean that one should strive for an excess of the rational faculty, as this is one of the causes of scepticism; rather, it means that we must be concerned with maintaining a balance. If a person is not rational enough, he can be too accepting and believe whatever he hears. This type of person can be easily deceived. Ibn Sinna, in a profound statement says "Whoever is used to accepting an argument without any reason is no longer a human being."[1] This is because a fundamental part of humanity is rationality and human being is often defined by philosophers as "rational animal". Therefore one needs to strike a balance, and not to be too rational and critical or too receptive.

2. The faculty of anger (*al-quwwah al-ghaḍabiyyah*) is the faculty that controls our temper. Without this faculty, we would not have the motivation to protect ourselves from danger. However, if someone allows this faculty to be extreme, they would be aggressive and always ready to attack. On the other hand, if a person lacks the faculty of anger they would be a coward. The philosophers in this school of thought encourage us to attain a balance between these two, so that

---

[1] The original text is as follows:

من تعود ان يصدق من غير دليل فقد انسلخ عن الفطرة الانسانية.

we can attain the virtue of bravery. A good person, therefore, is one who knows when to become angry and to the right extent.

3. The appetitive faculty (*al-quwwah al-shahwiyyah*) is the faculty which mostly consists of sexual appetite, but also includes our appetite for food and other things. If the force of sexual desire did not exist in man, the continued existence of the human species would be endangered. This faculty must also be brought to a balance where a person is chaste and modest.

Therefore, if one were to strike a balance in all these faculties he would have wisdom, bravery and chastity; this is all one needs to attain justice. This means that one who is just or *'ādil* is one who has attained perfection in every aspect of his soul. Being *'ādil* is not merely about abstinence from sins, but it is also about the perfection of every faculty.

This school of spirituality sets out a very rational response to the question of self-building. Although it is rational, some feel that it is too abstract and lacks the inspirational and emotional qualities that can really engage people and leave them motivated to change. We are taught to strike a balance with our faculties but it can be difficult to know where that balance is in different circumstances. This approach is useful, but not sufficient; we must add practical and inspirational elements to our view of self-building.

The Mystical Approach

The mystics consider the whole process of self-building as a journey towards Allah (swt) or perfection and as a matter of gradual growth. The difference between the previous approach and this approach is as follows:

According to the first approach, the relationship of the soul and self-building can be considered in the following way. Imagine there is a house which you wish to beautify; there are a number of things you could do. You could take out the rubbish, then start decorating the house, and furnishing the house in a wise way. If one manages to remove the rubbish and all the ugly items from the house, and furnishes it with beautiful items, then the house becomes attractive. In the same way we can consider the house which we wish to beautify as the soul we wish to cleanse and adorn with good character. We must remove bad qualities from our hearts in order for Allah (swt) to let the light in and furnish our hearts with a good character. For example, we read in a hadith, "angels do not enter a house in which dogs are kept".[1] In a similar way we must consider the state of our hearts, and if they are aggressive like a dog, ill tempered or diseased we cannot hope for angels to enter. Therefore, this process involves three main stages

---

[1] *Bihar al-Anwar*, vol. 56, p. 177. The original text is as follows:

قَالَ رَسُولُ اللَّهِ (ص): إِنَّ جَبْرَئِيلَ أَتَانِي فَقَالَ إِنَّا مَعْشَرَ الْمَلَائِكَةِ لَانَدْخُلُ بَيْتاً فِيهِ كَلْب.

- *Takhliyah* – clean out

- *Tahliyah* - adornment

- *Tajliyah* – starts shining (starts to happen automatically after you do first two).

Although this approach is inspiring to an extent, and can provide us with a framework through which to self-build, it is not a dynamic approach, as it does not fully explain where one should precisely start and finish the spiritual journey. It does not say what we should clean first or what to adorn ourselves with. Again, this approach is useful, but not sufficient in itself as a complete plan of self-building.

According to the second approach, the relationship of the soul and self-building can be considered in the following way. A person is like a flower, and a flower can grow but not without care. A flower can grow like any other that has grown in the past; it is not a unique thing. A flower is gradually growing if everything is carefully looked after. This is similar to how a child grows into an adult. One cannot be a teenager before being a toddler. In the same way, one cannot give the food of a toddler to a teenager or vice versa.

Therefore, the second approach i.e. the mystical approach looks at spiritual growth in a dynamic way as a carefully planned procedure. One needs the guidance of the people who have been to this process, who can provide advice for what to do at each stage. With this approach, every stage must be undertaken separately. This means that the expectations in each stage should be different. What is good for one person at one level may not be necessarily good for another person at a higher level. For example, if a small child memorises Surah *Al-Fatihah* (the Opening) and recites it people would commend the child and would be impressed, but if the Imam of the prayer recited the Surah in the same way, people would criticise him and not pray behind him. Everything is therefore a matter of comparison as to what we should expect from ourselves in different situations. It is a constant journey from one level to the next.

The Scripture/Text Based Approach

According to this view, the best approach is to refer to the Qur'an and Sunnah of the Holy Prophet (s) and his family (a). Those who advocate this approach therefore felt there was no need for a philosophical framework, and instead they listed the desirable and undesirable qualities of man based on the Qur'an. For example, for the vice of greed they would extract verses from the Qur'an which reveal that greed is an undesirable quality and provide evidence and some solutions from hadith.

What should be our own attitude?

All these scholars have made great contributions to Islamic moral thought. However, each of these approaches have their strengths and weaknesses and if we wish to benefit the most we must create a synthetic approach in which the advantages of each school of thought can be incorporated.

Requirements for an Adequate Approach

1. Our moral outlook should be compatible with the Qur'an and Sunnah, as there is no one better than Allah (swt) and the Holy Prophet (s) to guide, as to what is good or bad. All truth is from Allah (swt), no matter if it is relayed to us, by the mystics or the philosophers.

2. The ethical system has to be comprehensive. No aspect of the human being can be ignored. We do not want to have a person who is only developed in one aspect. A human being must grow in all different aspects.

3. The ethical system must be rational and supported by rational arguments, but it also must be practical and engaging.

4. The framework must be consistent and no contradictions should occur.

5. The ethical system must tell us what to do in different positions and stations as self-building is a dynamic process and is not static. In no field of study or practice can a person say they do not need consultation or advice.

6. Islam is a religion which considers reason to be very important. There is nothing irrational in Islam. There are many things taught by revelation, but this is not because they

are against reason; it is because they are above reason. To illustrate the difference between something being against reason and above reason let us consider an example. If someone was asked how many people are in the next room, using their reason alone, they could not tell you. This answer does not come through reason. However, if someone answered that there are one million people in the next room, knowing the size of the room, we could say that this answer is against reason.

Conclusion

We need a moral system based on the Qur'an and Sunnah, while at the same time has rational and philosophical grounds. The system must also have clear priorities, and if two things are in conflict, the system must show which is more important. Lastly, we must be able to find out what we can expect from each stage, usually by those who have passed the stage we are now in, as their advice and help is extremely important. Among our contemporary scholars, there have been brilliant teachers of spirituality who have combined these schools of thought, and whom we can learn from, such as: Imam Khomeini, Allamah Tabatabai, Ayatollah Mutahhari and Ayatollah Javadi Amuli.

Different Treatments of Spirituality[1]

In this essay we will study the ways the Qur'an and hadiths have treated the process of self-development and described man's effort and struggle to achieve piety and spirituality.

1. Spirituality as combat with the self: *According to this approach,* self-building is an internal battle against the enemy within. In a very well-known and inspiring hadith, we read that once, in Medina, Prophet Muhammad (s) saw a group of his companions who had won a battle approaching. The Holy Prophet (s) said:

مَرْحَباً بِقَوْمٍ قَضَوُا الْجِهَادَ الْأَصْغَرَ وَ بَقِيَ عَلَيْهِمُ الْجِهَادُ الْأَكْبَرُ قِيلَ يَا رَسُولَ اللَّهِ وَ مَا الْجِهَادُ الْأَكْبَرُ قَالَ جِهَادُ النَّفْسِ

Well done! Welcome to those people who have completed the minor struggle and on whom the greater struggle is still

---

[1] This essay is a revised version of a similar title published in the *Message of Thaqalayn*, vol. 10, no. 3.

incumbent." The Apostle of Allah was asked: "What is the greater struggle?" He replied: "To fight one's own self. [1]

The companions had defeated their enemies in a severe battle and had been prepared to give up the dearest thing to them, their life, to defend Islam. They were astonished and wondered what could be greater than that. The Holy Prophet (s) replied: '*Jihad al-nafs*.' This means to fight one's own self, to struggle with your own self.

In a well-known hadith Abu Dharr asked Prophet Muhammad (s): 'Which struggle is the best?' The Holy Prophet (s) replied:

أفضل الجهاد أن يجاهد الرّجل نفسه و هواه

To struggle against one's own self and lusts.[2]

The likening of self-development to an internal battle is indeed rooted in the Qur'an itself. For example, the Qur'an says:

وَ مَن جَاهَدَ فَإِنَّمَا يجُاهِدُ لِنَفْسِهِ إِنَّ اللَّهَ لَغَنِى عَنِ الْعَالَمِين

And whoever strives, he strives only for his own soul; most surely Allah is Self-sufficient, above (need of) the worlds. (29:6)

---

[1] *Al-Kāfi*, vol. 5, p. 12, no 3 and *Al-Amāli* by al-Saduq, Session 71, p. 377, no 8. There is an addition to the above hadith, which can be found in *Bihār al-Anwār,* vol. 67, p. 62 and reads as follows:

ثُمَّ قَالَ (ص): أَفْضَلُ الْجِهَادِ مَنْ جَاهَدَ نَفْسَهُ الَّتِى بَيْنَ جَنْبَيْهِ

The best struggle is to fight one's own self.

[2] *Nahj al-Fasāha*, p. 230,.

According to many exegetes of the Qur'an, this striving or struggle (*jihad*) which has been mentioned here is a spiritual jihad. There are two main pieces of evidence that they use to prove this. Firstly, the use of the word "himself": this is significant as in a war a soldier fights for a cause; it may be for the oppressed, for the dignity of Islam or for his country. However this verse mentions the cause as "himself." Secondly, previous to this verse Allah (swt) says:

مَنْ كانَ يَرْجُوا لِقاءَ اللَّهِ فَإِنَّ أَجَلَ اللَّهِ لآتٍ وَ هُوَ السَّميعُ الْعَليم

Whoever hopes to meet Allah, the term appointed by Allah will then most surely come; and He is the Hearing, the Knowing. (29:5)

This concept of meeting Allah (swt) is also a spiritual concept and so it is consistent with the following verse i.e. the verse 29:6 being about jihad for the self, as this too is a spiritual concept. Of course, this is not to suggest that this verse does not include the militant jihad, but that it also includes the spiritual jihad.

The following verses also refer to the spiritual jihad, though they may also include the militant jihad, since the militant jihad also needs purification of the intention and the soul:

وَ جاهِدُوا فِى اللَّهِ حَقَّ جِهادِهِ ...

And wage jihad for the sake of Allah, a jihad which is worthy of Him... (22:78)

وَ الَّذينَ جاهَدُوا فينا لَنَهْدِيَنَّهُمْ سُبُلَنا وَ إِنَّ اللّهَ لَمَعَ الْمُحْسِنينَ

And (as for) those who strive hard for Us, We will most certainly guide them in Our ways; and Allah is most surely with the doers of good. (29:69)

To fight an internal enemy is the greater struggle because it is more difficult. When an enemy is found inside it is more dangerous and more difficult to defeat. An internal civil war is more difficult to face than war against an external foreign enemy on one's borders. It is much more difficult to expel someone who has occupied our house than to repel someone who is only outside it. If our enemy is inside us then he knows all our secrets. He knows our weak points and our strong points and he knows exactly how to 'play' with us. An internal enemy is always with us and allows us no rest. We might be able to negotiate a cease-fire with an external enemy but with an internal enemy the fight goes on day and night, unceasingly. And unfortunately we love and admire this enemy because it is our own soul. He has done so many bad things to us and yet we still love him. So this is a very difficult and complex battle. We should be really determined and fully alert. Indeed, Allah should have mercy upon us if we are to win this battle.

We should know that, despite all the challenges to be faced in this struggle, in the end it is not so difficult. Allah will guide and make it easy for those who sincerely want it. It is very important that when we know something we must put it into practice. If we put our knowledge into practice, then Allah will give us knowledge of the things that we do not know. If we put into practice the small things that we know, it will enlighten the path before us.

2. Spirituality as a medicine.

Another approach is to consider spirituality as a kind of medicine for our soul or spirit. Spiritual problems are described as illness and so we need to treat ourselves with special medicines. We are patients in need of a cure, in need of medicine. Just like our bodies, our souls may also become ill. Unfortunately the most difficult sort of illness is when we suffer deep inside. In twelve verses, the Qur'an talks about a group of people who suffer from "disease in their hearts". This disease may be increased by Allah (swt) because they do not want to be cured and insist on being ill. For example, we read:

فى قلوبهم مرض فزادهم الله مرضا

In their hearts is a disease and Allah has increased their disease. (2:10)

The Qur'an also talks about hearts which are healthy and pure:

ولاتخزنى يوم يبعثون يوم لاينفع مال ولابنون الا من اتى الله بقلب

سليم

Do not disgrace me on the day when people are revived, the day on which neither money nor children can help, except the one who comes to Allah with a healthy (pure) heart. (26:87-89)

This is the prayer of the Prophet Abraham (a). In verses (37:83 & 84), Allah (swt) informs us that this request was granted: 'Indeed, Abraham was among his [i.e. Noah's] followers, when he came to his Lord with a healthy (pure) heart.'[1]

Thus, we can understand that having a pure and healthy heart is so important that someone like Prophet Abraham (a), the father of all monotheistic religions, asks Allah (swt) for it. Indeed, this is the only thing which will be useful on the Day of Judgement when neither children nor money will benefit us. In *Nah al-Balaghah*, sermon 388, Imam Ali says:

أَلا وَ إِنَّ مِنَ الْبَلاءِ الْفَاقَةَ وَ أَشَدُّ مِنَ الْفَاقَةِ مَرَضُ الْبَدَنِ وَ أَشَدُّ مِنْ مَرَضِ الْبَدَنِ مَرَضُ الْقَلْبِ

One of the catastrophes that may happen to a person is poverty, but more difficult than poverty is illness. And more difficult than illness of the body is illness of the heart.[2]

Therefore the worst poverty is to suffer from a lack of piety. The concept of medicine is also a very important related topic. Imam Ali (a) says in his Sermon of the Pious:

أَمَّا اللَّيْلَ فَصَافُّونَ أَقْدَامَهُمْ تَالِينَ لأَجْزَاءِ الْقُرْآنِ يُرَتِّلُونَهَا تَرْتِيلا يُحَزِّنُونَ بِهِ أَنْفُسَهُمْ وَ يَسْتَثِيرُونَ بِهِ دَوَاءَ دَائِهِم

---

[1] The Arabic text is as follows:

«وَ إِنَّ مِنْ شِيعَتِهِ لاِبْرَاهِيمَ إِذْ جَاءَ رَبَّهُ بِقَلْبٍ سَلِيمٍ»

[2] 2 *Nahj al-Balaghah*, p. 545

[Pious people are] those who stand up and recite the Qur'an at night, and they try to make themselves sad. They try to take from the Qur'an the treatment as medicine for their illnesses.[1]

Imam Baqir (a) told Jabir b. Yazid al-Ju'fi:

وَ اعْلَمْ أَنَّهُ لاعِلْمَ كَطَلَبِ السَّلامَةِ وَ لاسَلامَةَ كَسَلامَةِ الْقَلْبِ

And know that there is no knowledge like seeking health, and there is no health like the health of the soul.[2]

In the case of spiritual medicine, the most important point is that we must try to prevent illness from penetrating our souls, in the same way as we might try to maintain a distance from people who are ill, so that the disease does not affect us; by being close to them we endanger our own health. However, there are cures to our illnesses, as Allah (swt) is the Most Forgiving. Furthermore, we need a guide who can show us what to do and how to prevent or cure our illnesses. One of the beautiful things Imam Ali (a) mentions about the Holy Prophet (s) is that he was a doctor, but he did not wait for the sick people; instead he went to them himself, taking the equipment with him.

طَبِيبٌ دَوَّارٌ بِطِبِّهِ قَدْ أَحْكَمَ مَرَاهِمَهُ وَ أَحْمَى مَوَاسِمَهُ يَضَعُ ذَلِكَ حَيْثُ
الْحَاجَةُ إِلَيْهِ مِنْ قُلُوبٍ عُمْيٍ وَ آذَانٍ صُمٍّ وَ أَلْسِنَةٍ بُكْمٍ مُتَتَبِّعٌ بِدَوَائِهِ
مَوَاضِعَ الْغَفْلَةِ وَ مَوَاطِنَ الْحَيْرَةِ

---

[1] *Nahj al-Balaghah*, p. 303, Sermon 193.
[2] *Tuahf al-'Uqul*, p. 284.

> *The Prophet (s) was like a roaming physician who has set*
> *ready his ointments and heated his instruments. He uses*
> *them wherever the need arises for curing blind hearts, deaf*
> *ears, and dumb tongues. He followed with his medicines the*
> *spots of negligence and places of perplexity.*[1]

There were people who were deaf, blind, or those people who could not speak the truth, and the Holy Prophet (s) used the appropriate medicine to cure them. Imam Mahdi (a) who is the Imam of our age has also a significant role; and if Allah (swt) pleases we can receive guidance and healing from him (a).

3. Spirituality as a journey.

In Islamic literature, spirituality is also described as a journey. We should think of ourselves as wayfarers. We have all embarked on a journey away from Allah (swt) and then we are going back to Him. We have all been created by Allah (swt) and this creation is a sort of separation from our origin. Before we were created we were not separate from Allah (swt) but now we are. However, Allah (swt) has given us the chance to return to Him:

إِنَّا لِلَّهِ وَ إِنَّا إِلَيْهِ راجِعُونَ

Truly we belong to Allah and to Him we will return.
(2:156)

When we depart, our destination is clear. But in order to reach our destination we must be very careful about our direction. If we

---

[1] See *Nahj al-Balāghah*, p. 156, Sermon 108.

are on the right path, we will certainly reach our destination.
However, if we are on the wrong path, we will not reach our
destination and may even go farther and farther away from it.
We are not in a static or fixed position. Every day and every hour
we are moving and getting either further from or closer to our
destination. The Glorious Qur'an says:

يا أَيُّهَا الإِنْسانُ إِنَّكَ كادِحٌ إِلى رَبِّكَ كَدْحاً فَمُلاقيهِ

*O man, you are trying hard to reach your Lord and you will
finally meet Him.* (84:6)

Having read this verse, some may think that there is nothing to
worry about because we have all come from a good place and
there is a good destination ahead. But our status when we meet
Allah (swt) is of utmost importance. There are two states of
reaching Allah (swt): to reach Him while He is happy with us or
to reach Him while He is angry with us. Human beings are
among the very few creatures whose levels of perfection are not
fixed, that is, they have been given the capacity to upgrade or
degrade themselves.

Thus, the spiritual journey consists of trying to increase our
closeness and proximity to Allah (swt). It should be noted that
Allah (swt) is always close to us, but we are not necessarily close
to Him. We can reach a position in which we can get closer and
closer to Allah (swt) through self-purification, and, as suggested
by the Glorious Qur'an, "meet" Him. Mystics normally speak of
the possibility of losing our own selfhood, limits and boundaries
and then becoming identified with Allah (swt). I am not

commenting on this concept here, but in any case it seems obvious that we can get closer and closer to Allah (swt) to the extent that nothing will remain between us and Him and this is what we mean by returning to Allah (swt).

So this life is a journey and we cannot say that we do not want to go on this journey. We are all on this journey and it is up to us to gather enough provisions for ourselves. One of the main goals of self-building is to try to reduce this distance by wayfaring towards Allah (swt). The path towards Him is infinite and full of challenges. However, for the people who embark on this journey, all the support and guidance are provided. In this regard, Imam Sajjad (a) says:

سبحانک ما اضیق الطرق علی من لم تکن دلیله و ما اوضح الحق عند

من هدیته سبیله

May you be glorified! What a narrow path it is for whom You do not guide, and what a clear path it is for whom you have guided![1]

Conclusion: In this part we have discussed spirituality or the process of self-building as a kind of battle, medicine and as a journey. Allah (swt) is encouraging and guiding us demonstrating many anologies. He is showing us that there is always hope of reaching Him, and appeals to us in many different ways to encourage us to come closer to Him. He is the most merciful.

---

[1] *Bihār al-Anwār*, vol. 91, p. 147.

A Glance at the Process of Self-development[1]

The process of self-development has different stages. In what follows, I will try to study briefly the whole process and refer to its major stages.

1. Wakefulness or   attention to one's self: *The very first stage is* wakefulness (*yaqzah*), that is, to awaken from the pre-occupation of worldly engagements and to remove negligence. To awaken is to remember to look after one's piety, life and spirituality. Many scholars such as Imam Khomeini in his book: *Jihad-e Akhbar* (the Major Jihad), which is a compilation of lectures given by him to *Hawzah* students, state that the first stage of self-purification is wakefulness. Indeed some mystics believe that this is only a preliminary stage and that the first stage comes after wakefulness. However, there is no doubt that this is the beginning. The departure point is to become awake. We may say that we are all 'awake', but this is a different kind of wakefulness. According to a hadith, Prophet Muhammad said:

---

[1] This essay is a revised version of a similar title published in the *Message of Thaqalayn*, vol. 10, no. 4.

النَّاسُ نِيَامٌ فَإِذَا مَاتُوا انْتَبَهُوا

The people are asleep and only wake when they die.[1]

When they die, they wake and never go to sleep again. But then it is too late. Then they are like someone who wakes up when the train has gone, when the airplane has flown. At that time, there is no use or benefit in going to the airport because, although you are now awake, you have already missed the flight. All you can do is to blame yourself and be regretful. You might say that you will catch the next flight but unfortunately there are no more flights. It is the end of the world, that was the last flight and we missed it because we were asleep.

So, let us be awake. If we become conscious only when we die, we cannot do anything, as there is no opportunity to come back. Allah (swt) talks of the people who ask to be returned, so that they can do something good. He replies "this is just some words that this person says".[2] If he is given a chance, he will not change, and even then, there is no opportunity; they just wait for the day of resurrection. Unfortunately, death has become so familiar or naturalised that we do not think we are going to die, and it will always happen to someone else. According to an Iranian poet,

---

[1] *Biḥār al-Anwār,* vol. 50, p. 134.
[2] Chapter 23 verse 100. The Arabic text is as follows:

« لَعَلِّي أَعْمَلُ صَالِحًا فِيمَا تَرَكْتُ كلاَّ إِنَّهَا كَلِمَةٌ هُوَ قَائِلُهَا وَ مِن وَرَائِهِم بَرْزَخٌ إِلَىَ يَوْمِ يُبْعَثُون»

we are like a group of sheep, taken one by one to the slaughter house; each is enjoying, not thinking that they will be next.[1]

According to a hadith, the *Tawrah* of Moses says:

عَجِبْتُ لِمَنْ أَيْقَنَ بِالْمَوْتِ كَيْفَ يَفْرَح

"I am astonished that someone who is certain that he is going to die, can ever be happy".[2]

So we need to become alert and wake up before we die. Sometimes this happens through a significant event such as the loss of a relative, severe illness, or in meeting a pious person. However we should not wait for something to happen before changing; we can just change, as there is no guarantee that something will happen to us.

It is very easy to become awake: it just needs determination and for us to think about how important and significant this life, this journey to get closer to Allah (swt), is to us. This is the only chance that we have to obtain provisions for our eternal journey. According to a hadith, Imam Ali (a) said:

---

[1] *Divan Owhadi*, Qasideh no. 14:

«گرگ اجل یکایک از این گله می برد   وین گله را ببین که چه آسوده می چرند»

[2] *Irshād al-Qulub*, vol. 1, p. 74.

انّ اللّیل و النّهار یعملان فیک، فاعمل فیهما

Day and night are constantly affecting you so you should also try to affect them.[1]

This means that your life is passing by quickly. Every day and every night is making you older. In other words every day and every night is bringing you nearer to your end of life in this world, so try to do something.

There is a beautiful analogy regarding our situation. Life in this world is compared to a rope for a person who has gone into a deep well and is only holding onto that rope. If he loses this rope he will be finished. There are two mice, one white and one black, at the top of the well, gnawing on the rope. The time will come when the rope will definitely break. The mice are very determined and will not go away. This is our situation. The rope represents our life. The white mouse represents day and the black mouse represents night. Day and night are constantly 'gnawing' away at our life and sooner or later we will 'fall' and die.

So we must be awake and be very careful with this life, with this golden opportunity that has been given to us.

2. Knowing one's self: After becoming awake, we should try to find out what resources, opportunities and options are available to us. Now that we are awake, we want to do something. It is like someone who has no work or business and so has no source of

---

[1] *Ghurar al-Hikam*, p. 254, no. 329.

income. Everyone tells him to be responsible and do something. He agrees that he should do something but does not know what to do. He cannot start from nothing. First of all he should discover what kind of abilities and skills he has. He should know what options are available. For example, he should try to learn about the state of the business market. He should find out who has been successful so that he can take them as role models. He should also see who has become bankrupt so that he can learn lessons from their situation and avoid becoming like them. This is what is called 'self-knowledge' (*ma'rifat al-nafs*) and is considered to be "the most beneficial knowledge". Why do we always tend to forget about ourselves and know about other things instead? For example, there are some people who may spend all their life studying a rare species of insects but will not spend even one hour sitting down, trying to find out what Allah (swt) has placed inside them.

Muslim mystics say that there are two worlds: an external one consisting of the beautiful natural world of humans, animals, plants and non-living beings created by Allah (swt) and also an internal world inside our very selves. And they say that this world inside us is the greater world. What Allah (swt) has placed inside us is far greater than the whole physical world outside ourselves. This is why we read in a beautiful divine saying (*hadith-e qudsi*):

لَمْ يَسَعْنِى سَمَائِى وَ لاَ أَرْضِى وَ وَسِعَنِى قَلْبُ عَبْدِى الْمُؤْمِنِ

Neither my heaven nor my earth could contain Me, it is only the heart of a believing person that has contained Me.[1]

From this hadith, we can understand that our heart must be even greater than all these stars and planets, than this whole creation that we can see.

So, we need to know ourselves properly. We often underestimate the potential that we have for perfection. There is an endless possibility for perfection before us. Even the most holy people can still advance. There is always further for them to go because the distance between man and Allah (swt) is infinite and so there is always a possibility to go still higher. This is why we pray after *tashahhud*, "O Allah! Please accept the intercession of the Holy Prophet for us and also elevate his level". This means that the Prophet can go higher.

Many of us are too easily satisfied with our achievements. We need to be more determined and have greater expectations. If we are satisfied with small things, then we will lose out and maybe we will not even achieve those small things. It is said that once there was a religious scholar (*'âlim*) whose son had become a student of religion. The father asked his son what he wanted to become in the future. The son answered that he wanted to become like his father. The father replied that he felt very sorry

---

[1] *Bihār al-Anwār*, vol. 55, p. 39.

for his son because he himself had wanted to become as much as possible like Imam Ja'far Sadiq (a), who was his role model, and yet his present situation was all that he had achieved. He told his son that if he only wanted to become like his father then he would not achieve anything. So, we should always have great ambitions and indeed Allah (swt) has created us with such a potentiality inside us.

So, we need to know ourselves, we should believe in our potential and be aware of the different things that can benefit or harm us.

3. Taking care of one's self: After wakefulness and self-knowledge, we need self-care. It is not enough simply to know things; knowledge should serve us by being put into practice. For example, if you know that smoking kills but have no concern for your health and so continue to smoke, there is no benefit in that knowledge. In fact it just makes you more responsible and accountable because you know. Of course, this does not mean that we should avoid learning. To say we did not know is not a good enough excuse; we must learn and then put what we learn into practice. So we need to have self-care. The Qur'an states:

يا أَيُّهَا الَّذينَ آمَنُوا عَلَيْكُمْ أَنْفُسَكُمْ لا يَضُرُّكُمْ مَنْ ضَلَّ إِذَا اهْتَدَيْتُمْ إِلَى اللَّهِ مَرْجِعُكُمْ جَميعاً فَيُنَبِّئُكُمْ بِما كُنْتُمْ تَعْمَلُونَ

O believers, look after yourselves, if you are on the right path, you will not be harmed. (5:105)

To look after oneself implies practicing one's social responsibilities as well, since Islam is a religion that asks us to be actively engaged in social life: all with the spirit of wakefulness and consciousness, and knowing what can benefit and harm us.

However, there is something that often happens to people in this state. When they become conscious and sensitive to spiritual issues, then unfortunately instead of being concerned with their own piety, instead of being mostly busy with their own problems, they become judgmental about other people. For example, they start thinking that this person is useless, that one is careless and another one is not really a believer. This is very dangerous. First of all and most of all a true believer should be busy with his own problems. We understand from hadiths that it is much better for us if we are busy sorting out our own problems and illnesses rather than thinking about others and being judgmental. For example, the Prophet Mohammad (s) is quoted as saying:

طُوبَى لِمَنْ شَغَلَهُ عَيْبُهُ عَنْ عُيُوبِ غَيْرِهِ

Blessed is the one who is so busy thinking about his own deficiencies that he has no time to think about the deficiencies of others.[1]

Thus, we must start with criticising and assessing ourselves before looking at others. Sometimes we have an enormous problem within ourselves but we are not aware of it and yet we

---

[1] For example, see *Bihār al-Anwār,* vol. 1, p. 205.

notice a tiny amount of that same problem when it is in someone else. For example, we may have eaten something like garlic and do not realise that our mouth smells and yet when we meet someone who smells in some way, we are so quick to think or say something about them.

There is a story in *Mathnawi* by Rumi that four people had an appointment with a king immediately after midday prayers. They were very concerned not to lose this opportunity to meet the king and did not want to be late. So they decided to say their prayers quickly and then go to meet the king. They started praying as soon as they reached the mosque. However while they were saying their prayers, the one who calls for prayer (*mu'adhdhin*) came into the mosque to climb the minaret. They were now unsure and began to wonder whether they had started their prayers too early or whether that day the mu'adhdhin had arrived late. So, whilst praying, one of them asked the mu'adhdhin whether the time for prayers had already arrived or not. The second person asked the first why he had spoken whilst praying because whether the time had arrived or not he had now made his prayers void by speaking. The third person pointed out that the second person had now also spoken by asking the first one why he had spoken. However the fourth person considered himself to be "very clever". He said: 'Thanks to Allah (swt) that I did not speak!'

So, in this story we see that four people shared the same problem but each could only see it in the other people and not in themselves. In fact they repeated the very same mistake for which they were criticizing the others. Therefore it is so much better to be very concerned about ourselves rather than about other people. Sometimes people think that this means they should be indifferent to what is happening around them, in their community or in society. This is not the case. But if we want to be more useful to our community and to society then we should first start with ourselves and then we can help others. For example, we see that when giving instructions on a plane regarding the use of emergency oxygen masks, they always advise us to attend to ourselves first and then help those next to us. Otherwise, whilst we are trying to help the other person with their mask, we ourselves may collapse.

So, we should have self-care. But how should we care for ourselves? Should we only pray and recite the Qur'an? Should we just serve society by doing community work?

3.a.   Acquiring appropriate beliefs and faith: The very first thing that we need to do is to acquire proper beliefs and a proper understanding of the world. If you want to be a good businessman you must know the market and the people who are in the same business. You need to know the present situation, future possibilities and the factors that work in that particular business. If we want to be successful in this world we must know Who is the One who has control here. If we need to get permission to start a business we should know where to go to get that permission. In the same way, if we want to start a spiritual 'business' we should know from where to get permission. We should know what laws and regulations apply and should be observed. We should know what provisions are provided and what kind of loans and grants might be given to us.

Sa'di, a famous Iranian poet who wrote *Golestan* and *Bustan*, tells a beautiful story. He says that once a person went to do some business in another country. He realized that in that country the bell which they used to hang in the public bath-houses was very cheap to buy. For example, if the bell would have cost $100 in his country then in that country it cost only $1. So he sold all his goods and with whatever money he had, he purchased maybe a thousand bells. Then he expected to return to his country and generate $99 profit on each bell. So he transported all these bells back to his home town. However the problem was that there were only two or three bath-houses in his town and so no-one wanted to buy the bells. No-one was interested, even when he offered them at half price. So he lost all his capital and became bankrupt because he did not know which were the right kind of goods that would be purchased in his country.

Many people are like this and invest in things in this world which will be of no value in the hereafter. We invest our life, which is the most valuable 'capital' that we have been given, in things which, when we arrive in the hereafter, we will be told were pointless and thus we had wasted this 'capital'. Hence we need to have faith and to know the way in which our life in this world can secure our happiness in the next world. We must have correct beliefs and we should be especially careful to understand the connection between our life in this world and our life in the hereafter. About one third of the Glorious Qur'an talks about the hereafter. There is so much emphasis on it to teach us that the eternal life is the thing for which we must really prepare ourselves.

Another useful parable can be found in hadiths. There is an example in the story of the person who worshipped day and night: one day an angel passed by, thinking that with such dedication, this person must have a very high status. When the angel went close to him, he realised that the person did not have proper understanding of Allah, as he said "I wish you had a donkey so I could feed him in my field, as I have lots of grass here". This person saw Allah (swt) like a human being, who has a donkey. This kind of faith is not rewarding, and so *aqidah* is the first certainty that needs to be secured. We must make efforts to gain proper understanding of Allah (swt) the Creator, His position in this world, the belief in Unity, Prophethood, and Resurrection.

Therefore, first we should have correct beliefs, but not the kind of beliefs that we normally learn and can only repeat in a parrot-like fashion. It must be the kind of belief that we have completely absorbed into our very being so that if we say that there is only

One Allah, then our whole body and soul would declare that we are monotheist.[1]

3.b. Performing acts of piety and refraining from sins and evil deeds: We should try to perform our obligations and observe all the requirements of our faith. Even if we have proper beliefs and perform all our obligations but do not stop committing sins, we will not succeed. If someone washes his hands ten times a day but continues to touch things which are dirty and polluted, he will become dirty again. It is no use saying that he washed his hands ten times that day. Daily prayer is like a spiritual bath which makes us clean but if we do the same things again afterwards then we are just making ourselves dirty again.

There is a beautiful example of someone who has a carrier bag into which he puts some purchases in order to take them home. But there is a big hole in the bottom of the carrier bag and so whatever he puts into the bag falls out through the hole. He is surprised and wonders how it could be possible that he has filled the bag with at least ten times its capacity but it still remains empty. He wonders where everything is going. In a similar way, depending on our age, we have worshipped Allah (swt) for 10, 20, 30 or 40 years. But where is the result of this worship? Why are

---

[1] Being a good, kind and caring person is necessary but not sufficient to attain a place in heaven: we must also have faith. If people are good in their dealing with others, and have no faith, there is no chance to go to heaven: maybe they will not be sent to Hell, or their punishment will be reduced, but there is no way of attaining heaven. To believe in Allah (swt), as the One and only Creator is a necessary and fundamental belief.

we still the same kind of people? Why are we the same after the month of Ramadan as we were before it? It is because we do good things but in addition to this we also do bad things.

There is another useful example related by Rumi. There was a farmer who used to harvest his wheat and put it into his storeroom, hoping to fill it for the winter. But, to his astonishment, every time he went to the storeroom to fill it with more wheat he discovered that the level of the wheat would be lower than before and thus the storeroom was never filled. So he was surprised, especially as the storeroom was always locked so that no-one else had access to it to take anything out. He would always carefully lock the door. So he decided that one night he would have to stay awake inside his storeroom so that he could find out what was happening. So one night he indeed remained awake inside the storeroom, silently watching. After midnight he realized that there were some huge rats coming and taking all the wheat out of the storeroom. Thus he realized that they were the real cause of the problem. So Rumi tells us that we are like this. There are some rats in our hearts which take away the light of our good deeds. If there are no rats, then where is the light of forty years of praying, the light of forty years of fasting, of going for Hajj, etc.? So we should be very careful not to do any sinful actions. We should not commit even one single sin. Of course we are human beings and we may make mistakes, but a real believer is the one who, if he makes a mistake, firstly always feels sad and bitter about it and secondly he quickly repents and sincerely decides not to repeat the same mistake again. So, if we commit a sin we must repent as soon as possible.

Unfortunately, amongst some people who are interested in spirituality there are those who think that the religious law (*shari'ah*) is only needed at the beginning and that afterwards we should be concerned with the requirements of the spiritual journey (*tariqah*). Sometimes they say that this is like someone who has reached the core and so no longer needs the peel. But this is a wrong idea because we always need to observe the *shari'ah*. The Holy Prophet (s) and Imams of the Household of the Prophet (a) always followed the *shari'ah* and there is no one who can claim to be more pious than them. There is no incident where the Holy Prophet (s) committed a sin and then said that it was alright for him to do so. For example he never said that we should not tell lies but that it was allowed for him to do so. Or that we should not drink alcohol or gamble but that for him it was acceptable. Unfortunately nowadays we find that there are some so-called Muslims who follow people calling themselves masters or imams who do not themselves follow the requirements of piety and still their followers believe in them and think that they will never be affected by their unlawful deeds.

However, according to the school of Ahlul Bayt (a) this matter is very clear. We should observe the *shari'ah* but this is not enough. There are two different ways of looking at *shari'ah*. One is to believe that the *shari'ah* is only for the beginner and that after we reach the higher levels we no longer need it. This is what some

Sufis do. The second way is to say that the *shari'ah* is always needed but that by only following *shari'ah* we will always remain at the lowest level. If we want to go to the higher levels, in addition to the *shari'ah* we should try to go beyond the performance of mere rituals to discover the spirit contained within them. An example which might help is that of a person who is at primary school. If someone is at primary school and they feel satisfied with that, then their education will always remain incomplete. They need to go on to secondary school, to high school and then to university. But we cannot say that we will go to secondary school and once there we will forget about everything learnt at primary school. Or that when we go to university we will forget about everything learnt at high school. This will not work.

It has to be noted that nothing can replace performance of the obligations and refraining from the sins. In *Nahj al-Balāghah*, Imam Ali says (a):

لاتَكُنْ مِمَّنْ يَرْجُو الآخِرَةَ بِغَيْرِ عَمَلٍ وَ يُؤَخِّرُ التَّوْبَةَ بِطُولِ الأَمَلِ

Do not be one of the people who have hope for the hereafter without having good practice and who postpone repentance because he is too ambitious.[1]

If we maintain proper practice, little by little, the light of our deeds will enlighten our hearts. Even if you do little good things,

---

[1] *Nahj al-Balāghah,* p. 497, Wise Saying no. 146 (150).

it can be built upon, as long as you do not commit sins. Prophet Muhammad (s) told Abu Dharr:

يا أَبَاذَرٌّ يَكْفِى مِنَ الدُّعَاءِ مَعَ الْبِرِّ مَا يَكْفِى الطَّعَامَ مِنَ الْمِلْحِ يَا أَبَاذَرٌّ

مَثَلُ الَّذِى يَدْعُو بِغَيْرِ عَمَلٍ كَمَثَلِ الَّذِى يَرْمِى بِغَيْرِ وَتَرٍ

O Abu Dharr, with piety, you need to supplicate just the amount of salt you have on your food. O Abu Dharr, the example of the one who supplicates without practice is like the one who tries to shoot an arrow without rubber.[1]

On the other hand, if someone commits sins the performance of lots of good deeds will not help. We cannot compensate for sins with good deeds. The Qur'an says:

إِنَّما يَتَقَبَّلُ اللَّهُ مِنَ الْمُتَّقِينَ

Allah only accepts from the pious people. (5:27)

3.c. Acquiring good characteristics and removing bad ones:
In addition to having proper beliefs, performing our obligations and refraining from sins, we need to look into the qualities of our heart or spirit and find out what good qualities we lack so that we achieve them and what bad qualities we have so that we can remove them. This is what we normally learn in the science of *Akhlaq* (morality) and is much more difficult than having proper beliefs or proper practice. We often have bad habits which are difficult to change or even to notice, because they have almost

---

[1] *Bihār al-Anwār*, vol. 74, p. 83.

become part of us. In this situation we need to struggle and we need cure. For example a person may be fearful. As soon as it gets dark, they become frightened. Sometimes the person may be very determined to overcome this fear but it is still very difficult and needs some kind of treatment. Somehow it is like a cancer which needs difficult therapy. Firstly we must identify our bad habits and then we should try to promise ourselves that we will not do anything according to that habit because if we act according to a bad habit it becomes stronger and stronger. For example we may have a bad habit which we cannot remove immediately, but if we do not actually act according to that habit then gradually it becomes weaker and weaker. There are also specific solutions for particular bad habits depending on what kind of habits they are. So the general advice and solution is not to act according to a bad habit but also to apply specific solutions for the bad habits or qualities. For example if someone wants to stop smoking there are certain techniques to help break this habit which would not work for another habit.

Sometimes after decades you can become sure that you are good, and then you realise that you are bad. An example is someone who was always attending in the first row in the *jamaat* prayer, and after many years he realised it was not for the sake of Allah, since once when he came late and had to pray in the last row, he felt ashamed that people would think that he was not in the first row. He realised that it was for the praise of others that he was always early and in the first row. On the contrary, one may refer to an incident about Ayatollah Shaykh Mohammed Husayn

Isfahani Qarawi, the teacher of the late Ayatollah Khu'i. Once some people on a street in Najaf, saw that he was smiling and happy and someone asked him why he was happy. The Ayatollah replied that his bag of vegetables had fallen down, and when he started collecting them he was not concerned that people were looking at him. This made him happy, because he remembered another incident that had taken place in the early years of his study at the *hawza*. At that time he had an expensive *tasbih* as he was rich, and when it broke, he did not collect the beads since didn't want people to look at him. Now he felt content, that even though he was a great scholar, he did not feel bad that people were looking at him while he was picking up vegetables. At that point, he felt that there was no sense of pride in him.

In works such as *Mi'rāj al-Sa'ādah* and *Jāmi' al-Sa'ādah* we learn different faculties of our soul and the corresponding virtues and vices of each. We also learn the methods for obtaining the virtues and removing the vices.

3.d. Continuing the process of self-development until one becomes a true servant who meets his Lord: We should continue this process. It is a lifelong challenge which cannot be given a time limit of one month or one year or ten years after which time we could feel that we have completed it and allow ourselves to relax. On the contrary, as long as we remain in this world, up to the very last moment of our life, we must be careful. And we must not waste any opportunity. There is no age of retirement or graduation, because however much we manage to acquire, firstly it is not guaranteed that we will preserve them and secondly, even if we manage to maintain them, they will not constitute sufficient provision for our eternal journey. The Qur'an states, "And worship your Lord till certainty comes to you".[1] Before we meet Him, there is no sense of relaxation, retirement, graduation or rest. Insha Allah (swt) when we meet Him, then we can rest. So we must continue this process until we meet Him and He is happy with us.

There is an interesting story illustrating our situation. There was a group of people who were going to be sent to a dark tunnel. They were told that when they entered the corridor it would be very dark and they would not be able to see anything. They were told that they must go from one end of this tunnel to the other end and that on the floor there would be some stones which they could pick up and bring out. They were told that if they took the stones they would regret it, but that they would also regret it if they did not take the stones! Then they were sent into the corridor. Some people thought that it was not worth collecting the stones because they would regret doing so. Some others thought, out of curiosity, that they might as well take some stones to see what they were, even if they might regret it later. Thus some collected stones whilst others did not and then they all came out of the corridor. When they were outside again, in daylight, those people who had collected stones realised that they

---

[1] Chapter 15 verse 99. The Arabic text as follows:

«وَ اعْبُدْ رَبَّكَ حَتَىٰ يَأْتِيَكَ الْيَقِين»

were actually very expensive jewels. Those people who had not taken any stones saw this and became very angry. They started to protest, asking why they had been told that they would regret collecting the stones. Then they were told that although those people who do not collect any stones regretted this, even those who did take some regretted that they had not taken more and wished that they had collected more by filling their pockets as well.

So this is what we should do. We should make sure that our hands and pockets are overflowing with good characteristics and good deeds, get the benefit of them in this world and then take them to the hereafter.

Summary

There are various stages one must go through on the path of self-building. We must first awaken from our slumber of negligence and realise the reality of our existence: only then will we know ourselves and take care of our actions. This must be coupled with true beliefs and faith in the One Allah. Faith is not complete without good actions and so we must also refrain from forbidden acts. Lastly, we must rid our soul of bad qualities and habits. Although the path is difficult to embark upon, Insha'Allah (swt) with Allah's grace we shall gain the *tawfeeq* to complete these stages and achieve proximity to Him with ease.

Key Concepts in Islamic Spirituality:

Love, Thankfulness and Humbleness[1]

Love, thankfulness and humbleness are three very important or perhaps even the most important concepts in Islamic spirituality. In this essay, they will be discussed briefly. These three concepts are chosen not only because they are theoretically important, but also because they are practically rewarding. If we want to grow spiritually, we can easily do this by developing these qualities in our lives.

Love

According to Islamic hadiths supported by rational arguments, the entire reason for having faith or lacking faith is based on love for Allah (swt), and for whatever is related to Him (swt). For example, we read in hadiths that once the Prophet (s) asked his companions: "What is the strongest handhold in Islam?" The companions gave different answers: some said prayers, others said fasting and others hajj. After they gave their answers, they

---

[1] This essay is a revised version of a similar title published in the *Message of Thaqalayn*, vol. 11, no. 2.

said: "The Prophet and Allah know best". So the Prophet answered: "To love for the sake of Allah and to dislike for the sake of Allah."[1]

We must ask: what is the difference between one who is a believer and one who is not? It is not enough to know certain truths: Satan knows all those truths but he is still considered to be disobedient. Allah (swt) says in the Qur'an that there are people who know everything and yet disbelieve:

$$\text{... وَ جَحَدُواْ بِهَا وَ اسْتَيْقَنَتْهَا أَنفُسُهُمْ ظُلْمًا وَ عُلُوًّا}$$

They impugned them —though they were convinced in their hearts— wrongfully and defiantly... (27:14)

Similarly, to declare the truth is not sufficient to be a believer, as hypocrites declare the truth frequently. Describing such people, the Qur'an says:

$$\text{وَ مِنَ النَّاسِ مَن يَقُولُ ءَامَنَّا بِاللَّهِ وَ بِالْيَوْمِ الأَخِرِ وَ مَا هُم بِمُؤْمِنِين}$$

And there are some people who say: "We believe in Allah and the last day; and they are not at all believers." (2:8)

Love for the truth is the main distinction between a believer and a non-believer. Love requires knowledge and readiness to declare. This readiness to declare the truth does not include circumstances where a person must exercise *taqiyyah*, or the hiding of one's faith in order to safeguard his own life or the life of other believers.

---

[1] *Al-Kāfī*, vol. 2, pp. 125 & 126. The original text is as follows:

«أَوْثَقُ عُرَى الإِيمَانِ الْحُبُّ فِى اللَّهِ وَ الْبُغْضُ فِى اللَّه»

One might wonder why Islam focuses both on love for the sake of Allah (swt) and dislike for the sake of Allah (swt). One might question the need for disliking and say that we should only have love in our hearts. However, Islam is a rational religion, and it is rationally understandable that when we love something we must necessarily dislike its opposite. How can we love the honest without disliking the dishonest? Or love truth without disliking falsehood? If you love a virtue, you cannot help but dislike the vice. Similarly, if you love Allah (swt), you automatically dislike His enemies. Of course, a believer should not have any personal dislike for anyone. If we dislike someone, it is because of their bad qualities. We might love someone as the servant of Allah (swt), but we cannot love the bad qualities in him. This is the rational implication of loving good things.

Even if these two concepts are considered separately, they imply each other like two sides of the same coin. If we want to improve ourselves, we should try to increase our love for Allah (swt) and those who are close to Him, and increase our love for the acts which are loved by Allah (swt). This can be achieved by gaining more knowledge and then reflecting on it.

One interesting and practical way of improving ourselves is by reading biographies of people who have loved Allah (swt) immensely and developed a close relationship with Him (swt). Their life-stories reveal many hidden secrets about their lives, which can help and inspire us to be more inclined to their way of living. This is a naturally inspiring process.

Any knowledge that one gains must be coupled with reflection in order for that knowledge to come into practice. Reflection brings about a harmony in one's self, as one's emotions begin to support their knowledge. For example: if I know that telling lies is wrong, I might still tell lies. I need to take a few minutes every day and think about why telling lies is wrong, and realize, for example, that it brings about no benefit.

If we reflect on the people we love we may ask: why do we love these people? If someone gives you a job, you would not forget him for as long as you live; if someone teaches you something, you would be grateful and remember them; if someone helps you, or gives you money, or if your neighbour smiles at you or is kind to you, then you would love them. We do not need great reasons to love people: just a little caring and affection is enough. So how can we not love Allah (swt) when everything we have is from Him and nothing bad is from Him? We know these things, but we just need to reflect on them. If our love for Allah (swt) increases and intensifies, then we cannot disobey Him. How can you disobey the one that you love and make Him unhappy?

Love for Allah (swt) is therefore a very important concept which can help us practically to develop spiritually, and become closer to Him (swt).

Thankfulness

The virtue of thankfulness is very much related to love for Allah (swt). If you are thankful you will certainly love Allah because of

all His favours and if you love Allah you will believe in Him and
obey him. Thus, thankfulness is the core of *imān* (faith). It may
not be accidental that in Arabic the terms used to signify
ungratefulness and disbelief are identical, that is, kufr. Here are
some verses of the Qur'an where a contrast is made between
thankfulness and unthankfulness:

إِن تَكْفُرُواْ فَإِنَّ اللَّهَ غَنِيٌّ عَنكُمْ وَ لاَيَرْضَىٰ لِعِبَادِهِ الْكُفْرَ وَ إِن تَشْكُرُواْ
يَرْضَهُ لَكُمْ وَ لاَتَزِرُ وَازِرَةٌ وِزْرَ أُخْرَىٰ ثُمَّ إِلَىٰ رَبِّكُمْ مَّرْجِعُكُمْ فَيُنَبِّئُكُم
بِمَا كُنتُمْ تَعْمَلُونَ إِنَّهُ عَلِيمٌ بِذَاتِ الصُّدُورِ

*If you are ungrateful (takfur-u), indeed Allah has no need
of you, though He does not approve ingratitude (al-kufr) for
His servants; and if you give thanks He approves that for
you. No bearer shall bear another's burden; then to your
Lord will be your return, whereat He will inform you
concerning what you used to do. Indeed He knows best
what is in the breasts.* (39:7)

فَلَمَّا رَءَاهُ مُسْتَقِرًّا عِندَهُ قَالَ هَاذَا مِن فَضْلِ رَبِّى لِيَبْلُوَنِى ءَ أَشْكُرُ أَمْ أَكْفُرُ
وَ مَن شَكَرَ فَإِنَّمَا يَشْكُرُ لِنَفْسِهِ وَ مَن كَفَرَ فَإِنَّ رَبِّى غَنِيٌّ كَرِيمٌ

*So when he saw it set near him, he said, 'This is by the
grace of my Lord, to test me if I will give thanks or be
ungrateful (akfur). And whoever gives thanks, gives thanks
only for his own sake. And whoever is ungrateful (kafar)
[should know that] my Lord is indeed all-sufficient, all-
generous.'* (27:40)

وَ لَقَدْ ءَاتَيْنَا لُقْمَانَ الْحِكْمَةَ أَنِ اشْكُرْ لِلَّهِ وَ مَن يَشْكُرْ فَإِنَّمَا يَشْكُرُ لِنَفْسِهِ
وَ مَن كَفَرَ فَإِنَّ اللَّهَ غَنِيٌّ حَمِيد

*Certainly We gave Luqman wisdom, saying, 'Give thanks
to Allah; and whoever gives thanks, gives thanks only for
his own sake. And whoever is ungrateful (kafar), [let him
know that] Allah is indeed all-sufficient, all-laudable.'*
(31:12)

A very striking verse is to be found in the Chapter Man (76:3),
where thankfulness (to Allah for His guidance) is considered to
be identical with faith and to be unthankful is the opposite:

إِنَّا خَلَقْنَا الانسَانَ مِن نُّطْفَةٍ أَمْشَاجٍ نَّبْتَلِيهِ فَجَعَلْنَاهُ سَمِيعًا بَصِيرًا إِنَّا
هَدَيْنَاهُ السَّبِيلَ إِمَّا شَاكِرًا وَ إِمَّا كَفُورًا

*Indeed We created man from the drop of a mixed fluid so
that We may test him. So We made him endowed with
hearing and sight. Indeed We have guided him to the way,
be he grateful or ungrateful.* (76:2 & 3)

Therefore, *shukr* (thankfulness) is a very significant concept. It is
a primary issue related to the core of *imān*. It is also practical and
uncomplicated. Moreover, if we are thankful, we can achieve
many things as Allah (swt) says in the Qur'an:

وَ إِذْ قَالَ مُوسَى لِقَوْمِهِ اذْكُرُواْ نِعْمَةَ اللَّهِ عَلَيْكُمْ إِذْ أَنجَئكُم مِّنْ ءَالِ
فِرْعَوْنَ يَسُومُونَكُمْ سُوءَ الْعَذَابِ وَ يُذَبِّحُونَ أَبْنَاءكُمْ وَ يَسْتَحْيُونَ نِسَاءكُمْ
وَ فِي ذَالِكُم بَلاَءٌ مِّن رَّبِّكُمْ عَظِيمٌ وَ إِذْ تَأَذَّنَ رَبُّكُمْ لَئِن شَكَرْتُمْ
لأَزِيدَنَّكُمْ وَ لَئِن كَفَرْتُمْ إِنَّ عَذَابِى لَشَدِيد

When Moses said to his people, 'Remember Allah's blessing upon you when He delivered you from Pharaoh's clan who inflicted a terrible torment on you, and slaughtered your sons and spared your women, and in that there was a great test from your Lord.' And when your Lord proclaimed, 'If you are grateful, I will surely enhance you [in blessing], but if you are ungrateful, My punishment is indeed severe.' (14: 6 & 7)

Imagine a teacher who has a thankful student. That student appreciates the teacher and knows the teacher is doing a good job of helping him. Furthermore, the student declares that he is thankful, and then puts into practice what the teacher has taught him. The teacher would love to teach this student whatever he knows, as the teacher would not feel that his knowledge is being wasted. This is the example of a thankful servant who in his heart appreciates, with his tongue declares, and with his body, practices. Allah (swt) will give such a person more and more and He has no limits. The more He gives, the more you receive. In the *Dua* of *Iftitāh* we recite:

$$الَّذِى لاتَتْقُصُ خَزَائِنُهُ وَ لا تَزِيدُهُ كَثْرَةُ الْعَطَاءِ إلا جُودا وَكَرَما$$

O the one that whose treasuries never diminish and abundance of giving does not increase Him save generosity and bounteousness! [1]

One might wonder how it is possible that Allah's (swt) generosity increases by giving. When Allah (swt) gives you something and

---

[1] *Iqbal al-aʻmal*, vol. 1, p. 58.

you are thankful and can maintain that state, your capacity to receive increases. There is no limit for divine generosity except our limited capacity. The more Allah (swt) gives, the more capacity we have to receive, and so His Generosity accelerates into this infinite Mercy.

The concept of thankfulness has been explored by many Muslim scholars who have made various useful distinctions between the various types of thankfulness. According to Khājeh Abdullah Ansari in his book *Manāzil al-Sā'irīn* (The Stations of the Wayfarers), there are three main types of thankfulness:

- Thankfulness from the heart: knowing that something is a gift from Allah;

- Thankfulness with words: declaring that you are thankful for divine bounties;

- Thankfulness in practice: doing something with your hands, feet, eyes, etc., as acts of worship. This is practical thankfulness.

The first type of thankfulness is the most important, as it brings about the other two types. He also mentions that thankfulness consists of three main things:

- To know something is a gift: for example, one might know everything about health, but to know that health is a gift from Allah is to know something additional.

- To acknowledge that this is a gift from Allah: this means to admit that what one has been given is a gift, and that he/she is the recipient. Sometimes one might know something is a gift, but refuses to acknowledge it out of arrogance. One might think that he has earned it, or that he could live without it.

- To praise Allah for it.

Lastly, Khajeh Abdullah Ansari studies the notion of thankfulness and asserts that being thankful has different levels:

- Some levels are shared by ordinary people: they understand that there are some gifts from Allah that we are thankful for, and try to be pleased and praise Him.

- On higher levels, people are not only thankful for what they consider to be gifts that Allah has given them, but for whatever happens to them. Even a bad thing that occurs to a believer is not caused by a lack of love from Allah (swt), and so a believer is thankful for that.

- Some people are very concerned with Allah's presence: they feel no ease or pain as they do not have any time to think about whether they are in the state of ease or pain. This is the power of love. Similarly, if you are watching an interesting film, you might forget that you are hungry. Or if we are in the company of someone we love, we may forget the time and do not want the meeting to end.

People who love Allah (swt) to this extent are completely distracted and absorbed by His Essence. Khajeh Abdullah Ansari calls it the thankfulness of the elite.

Love and thankfulness are two intertwined concepts which can help us practically on our journey to self-improvement. Imam Khomeini in his book Forty Hadiths points out that the appearance of the effects of love and thankfulness become apparent in the heart, on the tongue and in the bodily acts and movements. As for the heart, one becomes filled with humility, awe and love. As for the tongue, the effects are among praise and glorification for Allah alone. As for the body, the effects consist of obedience and the use of the body for the sake of Allah. May Allah increase our love for Him by increasing our understanding of Him, and may He inspire us to be thankful in all situations.

Humbleness

Another key concept in Islamic spirituality is ultimate humbleness or spiritual poverty. This means to strengthen our understanding of the need for Allah and achieve a sense of complete reliance on Him. This means that even saying, "Allah has been very kind to me" or that "Allah has been very generous to me" is not enough. Who are we without Allah's favour and grace? We are nothing! It is not that Allah has been generous to something independent of Himself. We are nothing else than what He has created. All good things come from Him; in the best scenario we are just recipients, contingent creations of Allah, not independent from Him in any way.

One might compare this to humbleness: but it is more important, more intense, and at a higher level. Sometimes people try hard to be humble. For example, if they feel very important because they have been successful they try to control themselves so that they do not become arrogant; this is a struggle. But if one achieves spiritual poverty there is no need to struggle, as one would feel they had nothing of their own to be proud of except the gifts of Allah (swt). Reflection on our limits and absolute need for and reliance on Allah leaves no place for any kind of arrogance or self-admiration. Whatever we have, or is at our disposal, belongs to Allah. We are given things as trust for a short period of time and will be questioned on the Day of Judgement about the way we have dealt with them. Indeed, we ourselves belong to Allah in our very existence. Rene Guenon (1973) writes:

> *The contingent being may be defined as one that is not self-sufficient, not containing in himself the point of his existence; it follows that such a being is nothing by himself and he owns nothing of what goes to make him up. Such is the case of the human being in so far as he is individual, just as it is the case of all manifested beings, in whatever state they may be for, however great the difference may be between the degrees of Universal Existence, it is always as nothing in relation to the Principle. These beings, human or others, are therefore, in all that they are, in a state of complete*

dependence with regard to the Principle "apart from which there is nothing, absolutely nothing that exists"; it is the consciousness of this dependence which makes what several traditions call "spiritual poverty".

At the same time, for the being who has acquired this consciousness, it has, as its immediate consequence, detachment with regard to all manifested things, for the being knows from then on that these things, like himself, are nothing, and that they have no importance whatsoever compared with the absolute Reality.[1]

Imam Husayn (a) prays to Allah (swt):

فَبِأَيِّ شَيْءٍ أَسْتَقِيلُكَ يَا مَوْلاىَ أَ بِسَمْعِى أَمْ بِبَصَرِى أَمْ بِلِسَانِى أَمْ بِيَدِى أَمْ بِرِجْلِى آلَيْسَ كُلُّهَا نِعَمُكَ عِنْدِى

By which thing can I now meet You, O my Master? Can I come with my ears, my sight, my tongue, my hands, my feet? Is not this the case that all of these are your blessings that you have given me? [2]

Elsewhere Imam Husayn (a) says:

الهى انا الفقير فى غناى فكيف لا اكون فقيرا فى فقرى

O My Lord! I am poor in my richness so how can I not be poor in my poverty? [3]

---

[1] *Al-Faqr or Spiritual Poverty*, pp. 16-20.
[2] *Bihar al-Anwar*, vol. 95, p. 222.
[3] Ibid., p. 225.

Whatever I have is a sign of my need, a sign of my dependence. What about that which I do not have? Suppose that there is a person who has taken a loan, say, of one million dollars from a bank and another person who has taken one hundred thousand dollars. Which one is richer, and which one is not? It seems obvious that the one who has taken more money is more indebted and more responsible and must have more concerns and worries. Whatever Allah (swt) gives us puts us more in debt. There are many many things that we do not have and even those things that we have do not belong to us so how can we feel proud and free from needs. Imam Husayn (a) says:

$$ أَنَا الْجَاهِلُ فِى عِلْمِى فَكَيْفَ لاأَكُونُ جَهُولا فِى جَهْلِى $$

With respect to my knowledge, I am ignorant. How can I not be very ignorant in respect to what I do not know? [1]

What we know is very limited and surrounded with lots of questions. The more we know, the more questions we will have. This is why those who are more knowledgeable are more careful and cautious in their claims and farther from arrogance. Also, over time, we can easily lose what we know. There are people who cannot even remember their own names or the names of their closest relatives. Imam Husayn (a) also says:

$$ إِلَهِى إِنَّ اخْتِلافَ تَدْبِيرِكَ وَ سُرْعَةَ طَوَاءِ مَقَادِيرِكَ مَنَعَا عِبَادَكَ $$
$$ الْعَارِفِينَ بِكَ عَنِ السُّكُونِ إِلَى عَطَاءٍ وَ الْيَأْسِ مِنْكَ فِى بَلاءٍ $$

---

[1] Ibid.

O Allah! Verily the alteration of your affairs and the speed of progress of your decrees prevent those servants of You who know You to be confident when faced with your favour or to feel despaired when challenged with calamities. [1]

Everything changes quickly in this world. Sometimes we are happy and sometimes sad. Sometimes people respect us and sometimes no one respects us. Sometimes our children are good to us and sometimes not. There are lots of ups and downs. What is the reason for this? We need to learn that we cannot trust anything except Allah (swt). No one knows what will happen and, therefore, we should not trust anything. As the sayings of Imam Husayn (a) shown above teach us, we should not trust anything or anyone other than Allah (swt) and at the same time we should not despair. We should not be hopeless or feel helpless when bad things happen. The key is in the hands of Allah (swt) and He can change our situation to betterment in any moment. Having said all this, Imam Husayn (a) says:

أَنَا أَتَوَسَّلُ إِلَيْكَ بِفَقْرِى إِلَيْكَ وَ كَيْفَ أَتَوَسَّلُ إِلَيْكَ بِمَا هُوَ مَحَـالٌ أَنْ
يَصِلَ إِلَيْكَ أَمْ كَيْفَ أَشْكُو إِلَيْكَ حَالِى وَ هُوَ لاَيَخْفَى عَلَيْكَ

I appeal to You with my poverty and need for You. And how can I appeal to You with something which is impossible to reach You? Or how should I mention my complaint to You while it is not hidden to You? [2]

---

[1] Ibid.

[2] Ibid.

إِلَهِى كَيْفَ لاأَفْتَقِرُ وَ أَنْتَ الَّذِى فِى الْفُقَرَاءِ أَقَمْتَنِى أَمْ كَيْفَ أَفْتَقِرُ وَ أَنْتَ
الَّذِى بِجُودِكَ أَغْنَيْتَنِى

*O my Allah! How can I not be poor when You have put
me amongst the poor? And how can I be poor when you
have made me rich with your generosity?*[1]

This shows that the means (*wasilah*) that the Imam (a) uses to get
closer to Allah (swt) is his dependence on Allah (swt) and his
deep understanding that he is poor and nothing before Allah
(swt). Thus, the valuable means that Imam Husayn (a) finds and
wants to use is 'poverty'. According to the Qur'an, we are all
needy. The Qur'an says:

يَـٰأَيُّهَا النَّاسُ أَنْتُمُ الْفُقَرَاءُ إِلَى اللَّهِ وَ اللَّهُ هُوَ الْغَنِى الْحَمِيد

*O mankind! You are the ones who stand in need of Allah,
and Allah—He is the All-sufficient, the All-laudable.*
(35:15)

We are all needy and it is only Allah (swt) who is rich and free of
need. Many people do not understand this. Imam Husayn (a)
declares that he understands and admits this and wants to use it
as a means to get nearer to Allah (swt). Then the Imam (a)
describes that when he wants to come with his poverty there is a
problem, in that poverty does not reach Allah (swt). This is to
emphasise that poverty is only from one side; poverty cannot
reach Allah (swt). This may also mean that the one who goes with

---

[1] Ibid. p. 226

poverty will meet Allah (swt) whilst he is rich. To become rich you must take poverty with you, but the people who feel that they are the poorest people are the richest people in the eyes of Allah (swt). Whoever is the most humble, Allah (swt) will raise him more than anyone else. As we find in a hadith, 'whoever tries to be humble for Allah's sake, Allah (swt) will elevate him.'[1] In a divine saying (*Hadith Qudsi*) we find that Allah (swt) told Moses (a) the reason why He made him a Prophet is that He looked into the hearts of all people and saw that Moses was the most humble one. [2]

According to a well-known hadith, the person who avoids arrogance and chooses to be humble before Allah (swt) and serves Him sincerely is no longer a slave of others or of his own whims. He will achieve some kind of lordship:

الْعُبُودِيَّةُ جَوْهَرٌ كُنْهُهَا الرُّبُوبِيَّة

The servitude to Allah is a substance whose essence (core) is the lordship.[3]

In another hadith, we read:

---

[1] This hadith is narrated from Jesus (*Bihār al-Anwār*, vol. 14, p. 307), Prophet Muhammad (s), (vol. 16, p. 265; vol. 72, p. 120), Imam Sadiq, (vol. 72, p. 121) and Imam Kadhim (vol. 75, p. 312). The original text is as follows:

«مَنْ تَوَاضَعَ لِلَّهِ رَفَعَه»

[2] *Ithbat al-Wasilah*, p. 55. The original text is as follows:

قال له: يا موسى أ تدرى لم اصطفيتک على الناس بوحيى و کلامى؟ قال: لا يا رب.

قال: انى قلبت عبادى ظهرا لبطن فلم أر منهم أذلّ نفسا لى منک

[3] *Misbah al-Shari'ah*, p. 7.

عبدى أطعني اجعلك مثلى أنا حى لا أموت، اجعلك حيّا لا تموت،

أنا غنى لا أفتقر أجعلك غنيّا لا تفتقر، أنا مهما أشاً يكن أجعلك مهما

تشأ يكن

My servant, obey Me. [If you do so] I will make you an example of Myself. I am alive and never die so I make you alive and never die. I am rich and never become poor so I make you become rich and never poor. Whatever I want it will be, so I make you in the way that whatever you want it will be there.[1]

Reflecting on his life, one can see in Prophet Muhammad(s) the perfect example of humbleness. Indeed, the reason why Prophet Muhammad (s) was chosen to be the 'Seal of the Prophets' and was given the final message of Allah (swt) lies mostly in the fact that he was a true servant of Allah (swt) and the most humble person before Allah (swt) and His people. At least nine times a day in their prayers Muslims bear witness that Prophet Muhammad (s) was a servant of Allah (swt) and His Apostle. This means that among all his qualities there are two that are exceptional: first, he managed to be a servant of Allah (swt) and second, he was rewarded by being appointed as the Apostle of Allah (swt).

The Prophet (s) was so humble that he never admired himself; he never felt superior to others. He never separated himself from the masses and always lived a very simple life. He maintained the

---

[1] *Al-Jawāhir al-Saniyyah fi al-Aḥādith al-Qudsiyyah*, p. 284.

same conduct while he was both alone and powerless as well as when he ruled the Arabian Peninsula and Muslims were whole-heartedly following him. He lived very simply and was always with the people, especially the poor. He had neither a palace nor guards. When he was sitting with his companions, no one could distinguish him from others by considering his seat or clothes. It was only his words and spirituality that distinguished him from others.

Just before his demise, the Prophet (s) announced in the Mosque: "Whoever among you feels that I have done injustice to him, come forward and do justice. Surely, enacting justice in this world is better in my view than being taken account of in the Hereafter in front of the angels and the Prophets." Those present in the Mosque wept, for they were reminded of all the sacrifices that the Prophet (s) had made for them and the troubles that he had undergone in order to guide them. They knew that he never gave any priority to his own needs and never preferred his comfort and convenience to others. They therefore responded with statements of deep gratitude and profound respect. But one among them, Sawadah b. Qays, stood up and said: "May my father and mother be your ransom! O Messenger of Allah! On your return from Ta'if, I came to welcome you while you were riding your camel. You raised your stick to direct your camel, but the stick struck my stomach. I do not know whether this strike was intentional or unintentional." The Prophet (s) replied: "I seek refuge from Allah *(swt)* from having done so intentionally."

The Prophet (s) then asked Bilal to go to the house of Fatimah (a) and bring the same stick. After the stick was brought, the Prophet (s) told Sawadah to retaliate by hitting him back. Sawadah said that the stick had struck the skin of his stomach. The Prophet (s) therefore lifted his shirt so that Sawadah could in return strike his skin. At that moment, Sawadah asked: "O Messenger of Allah! Do you allow me to touch my mouth to your stomach?" The Prophet (s) gave him permission. Sawadah then kissed the stomach of the Prophet (s) and prayed that because of this act of his, Allah *(swt)* would protect him from fire on the Day of Resurrection. The Prophet (s) said: "O Sawadah! Will you pardon me or do you still wish to retaliate?" He replied: "I pardon you." The Prophet (s) then prayed: "O Allah! Pardon Sawadah b. Qays as he pardoned Your Prophet, Muhammad!"[1]

Thus, in Islamic spirituality it is very important to feel humble and that we are nothing in front of Allah (swt). Not just as a claim that we may utter without firm belief, but as a deep sense of nothingness. Once a person saw Imam Sajjad (a) in Masjid al-Haram, next to Ka'bah at Hijr of Isma'il. He said: 'I went to Hijr Isma'il and saw Ali b. Husayn (a) there saying his prayer. Then he went for Sajdah (prostration). I told myself: this is a pious man from a pious family, so let me listen to him while praying in his Sajdah.' Then he quoted the Imam (a) as praying:

$$\text{عُبَيْدُکَ بِبَابِکَ أَسِيرُکَ بِفِنَائِکَ مِسْكِينُکَ بِفِنَائِکَ سَائِلُکَ بِبَابِکَ}$$

---

[1] *Mustadrak Wasā'il*, vol. 18, pp. 287 & 288.

*My Lord, your small and little servant has come to your
door, your captive has come to your door, the one who is poor
has come to your door, the one who begs you has come to
your door.*[1]

In the Qur'an, Allah (swt) warns the believers that if they turn
away from His religion, Allah (swt) will soon bring forward a
people that among their characteristics is their humbleness before
the believers:

يَـٰٓأَيُّهَا الَّذِينَ ءَامَنُواْ مَن يَرْتَدَّ مِنكُمْ عَن دِينِهِ فَسَوْفَ يَأْتِى اللَّهُ بِقَوْمٍ
يُحِبُّهُمْ وَ يُحِبُّونَهُ أَذِلَّةٍ عَلَى الْمُؤْمِنِينَ أَعِزَّةٍ عَلَى الْكَافِرِينَ يُجَاهِدُونَ فِى
سَبِيلِ اللَّهِ وَ لَايَخَافُونَ لَوْمَةَ لَائِمٍ ذَٰلِكَ فَضْلُ اللَّهِ يُؤْتِيهِ مَن يَشَاءُ وَ اللَّهُ
وَاسِعٌ عَلِيمٌ

*O you who have faith! Should any of you desert his religion,
Allah will soon bring a people whom He loves and who love
Him, [who will be] humble towards the faithful, stern
towards the faithless, striving hard in the way of Allah, not
fearing the blame of any blamer. That is Allah's grace
which He grants to whomever He wishes, and Allah is All-
bounteous, All-knowing.* (5:54)

In Islamic literature, especially that by Persian poets, great
emphasis has been put on spiritual poverty. For example, in a
long poem in his *Mathnawi*, Rumi illustrates the significance of
this feeling of nothingness and humility and the fatal danger of
pride and arrogance. Rumi argues that whomsoever people flatter

---

[1] *Bihār al-Anwār,* vol. 96, p. 196.

and prostrate before indeed poison him. If he is not spiritually strong, he may be deceived and feel proud of himself. In this way, he may become arrogant and damage himself and lose his humility. When people flatter someone who is clever he will realize that this can be detrimental. Rumi goes on praising those who are humble in contrast to those who are arrogant. The example of someone who has not established humbleness in himself is like the one who drinks a poisonous wine. In the beginning he may feel happy and joyful, but after a few minutes he will collapse.

Another example that Rumi provides is the fight between two kings. When one king wins the battle and becomes victorious he will either imprison the defeated king or kill him, but he will never punish the beggars or the poor subjects of the defeated country. Indeed, he may help and promote them. Rumi says that the reason is that these types of people are humble and have no ambition of becoming a king and therefore they do not pose a threat to the new king. Another example is a caravan which is going from one place to another. When the thieves come to rob the caravan, those who have no money will be safe. Or when wolves attack they may attack anything that comes before them. They may even attack each other and this is why when they want to sleep they sit in a circle so that they can carefully watch each other. But Rumi says if there is a dead wolf they will not attack him. We know that the Prophet Khiḍr made a hole in the bottom of a boat because there was an unjust ruler in that area who used to confiscate every boat or ship passing by. Thus, the only way for that boat to be saved was to make it unusable. If a mountain or hill has lots of valuable minerals inside, people will excavate the area to bring out all the soils, sand and minerals out of it. But an ordinary hill or mount which has nothing special inside will remain intact. Someone who is walking is standing on his feet and his neck is straight. Therefore, the enemies may cut off his neck with their sword, but no one would cut off the head of a shadow person, since the shadow is so "humble" that no one thinks that it may pose any threat. When a ladder is going to collapse the one who climbs higher is very stupid. When the ladder collapses his bones will be damaged more severely.

After mentioning these examples, Rumi finally asserts that whatever he said were like the branches whose root or principle is much deeper. The underlying principle is that to feel arrogant is to associate one's self with Allah (swt). This is polytheism (*shirk*). Rumi goes on saying that since you have not yet died and again gained life through Allah (swt), you are not enjoying a spiritual life. Without such a death, whatever position you take is shirk. But if you die and become selfless, that is, if you are revived through Allah (swt) you may go higher and higher. In such condition, whatever you possess is for the sake of Allah (swt) and will be spent for the sake of Allah (swt). This is pure tawhid or monotheism.[1]

---

[1] This section of Rumi's poem starts with the following couplets:

تو بدان فخر آوری، کز ترس و بند   چاپلوست گشت مردم، روز چند

It has been suggested that poverty means to not possess something and at the same time to have the desire to possess it. For example, he who feels in himself a certain lack of human perfection and sincerely desires to remedy this lack is a '*faqir*'. Furthermore, it has been suggested that in Sufism "the longing of love is born of *faqr* (spiritual poverty)."[1] I think there are some problems with this understanding of poverty. First, poverty is much more than not to possess and then desire to possess. I think poverty is an awareness of our absolute need and dependence on Allah (swt) and as long as we are what we are this need cannot be removed. Second, this sense of poverty is a spiritual gift and virtue that should be maintained forever. Poverty is not a transient station towards richness or affluence. Rather, poverty itself is the greatest wealth and fortune that human beings can ever have. Prophet Muhammad (s) said:

اَلْفَقْرُ فَخْرِی وَ بِهِ أَفْتَخِرُ عَلَى سَائِرِ الْأَنْبِیَاء

My honour is from spiritual poverty. I have been honored over and above all prophets by being graced with spiritual poverty.[2]

هر که را مردم سجودی میکنند   زهر اندر جان او می آکنند

And ends with these couplets:

این فروع است و اصولش آن بود   که ترفع، شرکت یزدان بود

چون نُمُردی و نگشتی زنده زو   یاغیی باشی، به شرکت، مِلک جو

چون بدو زنده شدی، آن خود وی است   وحدت محض است، آن شرکت کی است ؟

[1] *Spiritual Poverty in Sufism.*
[2] *Biḥār al-Anwār,* vol. 69, pp. 32 & 55.

Conclusion: In this essay, we have discussed the concept of love as the strongest foothold in Islam, and as a distinguishing factor of a true believer. Knowledge, coupled with reflection and the grace of Allah (swt), can increase our love. Secondly, we discussed the concept of thankfulness as equal to faith, as taught in the Qur'an. Understanding the different levels of thankfulness can help us to be aware and thankful in all situations.

In this essay, we also discussed humbleness and spiritual poverty, through which one can attain piety, spirituality and alleviation from worries and difficulties. This concept is not implying that human beings have no value, and neither does it underestimate the value of human beings; rather, it fully appreciates the value of humans: by serving the Most Perfect and the Most Pure Allah (swt), we can get closer and closer to perfection.

May Allah (swt) help us understand how much we need Him, how much He has given us, how to really ask from Him in the best way, and how to make Allah (swt) pleased with us so we can become enlightened and pure. Allah (swt) has all the power and all the reasons to be kind to us, and if there are any obstacles, they are only due to us.

> *O Allah, grant me*   *the riches of poverty*
> *for in such largesse lies*   *my power and glory*[1]

---

[1] *Hafiz*

Practical Instructions for Spiritual Journey[1]

We have already discussed some general principles, such as observing the shari'ah and taking care of our qualities and characteristics.[2] However there are also certain practices which can strengthen us, increase our will-power and which can make us courageous and determined enough to continue the spiritual journey. These should then keep us on the right track.

There are five instructions given by all Muslim mystics which are indeed rooted in the Qur'an and the Sunnah.

1. Not to speak unless necessary

We should try not to speak too much. People may think that this is not very important but in fact it is very important indeed. We should try to speak only as much as it is necessary. Unfortunately there are many types of sins that are committed by people which are related to the tongue. Some scholars have counted up to

---

[1] This essay is a revised version of a similar title published in the *Message of Thaqalayn*, vol. 11, no. 1.
[2] Please refer to the essay, "A Glance at the Process of Self-development"

seventy types of such sins. Once a person requested the Prophet Muhammad (s) to give him some advice:

قَالَ لَهُ رَجُلٌ أَوْصِنِى فَقَالَ لَهُ احْفَظْ لِسَانَكَ ثُمَّ قَالَ لَهُ يَا رَسُولَ اللَّهِ

أَوْصِنِى قَالَ احْفَظْ لِسَانَكَ ثُمَّ قَالَ يَا رَسُولَ اللَّهِ أَوْصِنِى فَقَالَ وَيْحَكَ وَ

هَلْ يَكُبُّ النَّاسَ عَلَى مَنَاخِرِهِمْ فِى النَّارِ إِلَّا حَصَائِدُ أَلْسِنَتِهِمْ

The Prophet (s) said: "Keep your tongue!" Again the man requested for advice. The Prophet (s) said: "Keep your tongue!" For the third time the man asked for advice. The Holy Prophet said: "Ah, is there anything other than what people collect with their tongues that causes to collapse on their faces in the fire?" [1]

One reason that speaking can be the cause of so many sins is because we always speak. We continually speak because it is easy for us. We do not need to make any effort; nor do we need any instruments, means, training or money; and for this reason we have less control over what we say. Nowadays, it is even easier to speak to each other, as many alternative methods of communication have become widely available, enabling people in different countries to communicate, and therefore leaving more opportunity for sin.

In early Islam, some people used to put some sand in their mouths in order to make it more difficult to speak. If they had ever thought of something to say, they would have had to first remove the sand. By the time they thought about doing this, they

---

[1] *Bihar al-Anwar*, vol. 74, p. 159.

thought about the need for speaking and about what they were going to say, and realised it was better not to speak. This reduced the amount of unnecessary talk. This is not what I advise to do, and I only relay this story to emphasise my point that it is necessary to control what we say.

Even if what we say is not prohibited (*harām*) we should still not say it unless it is necessary. Unnecessary talk is harmful to our spirituality. Our words not only make our minds preoccupied, but also have great impact on our hearts. It is like when someone eats too much of a poisoned food. Not only would he have pain in his stomach because he cannot digest the food properly, but also he would become ill and feel sick. Our hearts become ill from saying things which are unnecessary. From a spiritual point of view, there is no single act or word, except that it either brings light or darkness. Unnecessary talk or speech is harmful and makes our heart dark.[1] We should take this very seriously as it is of utmost

---

[1] Some people may wonder why they do not feel darkness of the heart when they speak too much or even when they speak sinfully like backbiting (*ghaybah*). The answer is that sensibility of people is very different. You may recall the story about the perfume market from *Mathnawi* by Rumi which was mentioned earlier in this book. There was a person who brought a horse to a perfume market. The horse made the market dirty. This made the perfume-sellers very upset, as previously the market had beautiful aromas filling every corner. They wanted to get the market cleaned, but no one could tolerate going near the bad smells. They decided to hire someone who was accustomed to these bad smells so they found a young man whose job was to clean and wash horses. They brought him to the market, but as soon as the perfume fragrances reached the man, he fainted as he could not tolerate the scents. This is because his tolerance for scents had been transformed. In the same way, there are people who are used to dirt: physical or spiritual. Not only are they used to

importance. If we can say something in five sentences rather than ten, then we should do this. If we were about to say something and then we realise that it is not necessary to say it, then it is better not to speak.

People may say that they have to sit with their parents, family or friends and that they must be sociable. In these circumstances we should of course say something but we must watch carefully what we do say and speak for the sake of Allah (swt). We can say to Allah (swt) that we are speaking in order to make our family or friends happy. 'To bring joy to the heart of a believer' is an act of worship. However, there is a huge difference between someone who says something to make others happy and a person who makes a mockery of others or who just wants to amuse himself or show off by saying too much.

So, we should watch our words carefully. There is a very interesting hadith from the Holy Prophet (s) which indicates that he told a group of his companions:

---

dirt, they are allergic to purity. So if we do not feel that something is bad, or we do not feel that our heart has been darkened, it is not because good things have no effect; rather, it is because our hearts have become desensitised. This is similar to a person who has a cold, and cannot taste food properly. Furthermore, sometimes very delicious food tastes bitter to him: this is not because the food is bitter; but because he has a distorted sense of taste.

لولا تكثير فى كلامكم و تمريج فى قلوبكم لرايتم ما ارى و لسمعتم ما
اسمع

*If it were not because of speaking too much and because of
those bad thoughts which come to your heart, you would
have been able to see what I see and hear what I hear.*[1]

This shows that, either we speak too much or we think about
things which are not useful and therefore we cannot make any
progress. It can be both easy and difficult not to speak. It can be
easy because there is nothing to learn, there is nothing we have to
buy and no special place is needed in order to implement this
advice. We are not required to do anything. We are just told not
to speak too much. So it seems that it is not difficult. But if we
try, we will find that it is indeed very difficult. Sometimes we may
feel as if we are going to explode because we want to say
something very much. But if we practice, it becomes easier.

According to some hadiths, silence is a very good form of
worship. For example, Imam Ali (a) is quoted as saying:

أَفْضَلُ الْعِبَادَةِ الصَّبْرُ وَ الصَّمْتُ وَ انْتِظَارُ الْفَرَجِ

*Patience, silence and awaiting faraj (delivery; relief) are best
types of worship.*[2]

---

[1] Cited from Sunni sources in *Al-Mizan fi Tafsir al-Qur'an*, vol. 5, p. 270.
[2] *Bihar al-Anwar*, vol. 68, p. 96.

لا عباده كالصمت

There is no worship like silence.[1]

الصمت روضه الفكر

Silence is the garden for contemplation.[2]

This is because when one is silent their mind starts to enjoy the beauty of the spiritual world. But if one speaks, their mind becomes busy with the physical world.

2. Not to eat more than necessary

In the same way as keeping silent, eating small portions affects the spirit in a powerful way, as it allows the spirit to grow. On the other hand, when we eat too much, even if our food is halal, it makes us busy and our spirit lazy. We will not be able to remain alert. In other words what we eat is food for our body, but fasting is food for our soul. However there is a dilemma here because we need to feed both our body and our soul as they both need food and we must give each of them its due right. What should we do? We should eat only as much as is needed for our health and in this way we can make sure that we have done justice to both our body and soul. Eating too much harms both our body and spirit. Fasting is very important and useful if we can do it, but even if

---

[1] *Ghural al-Hikam wa Durar al-Kalim,* p. 768.
[2] Ibid. p. 37.

we do not fast we can achieve a great deal by simply reducing the amount of food we eat. One practical way of implementing this is shown to us by Allamah Tabataba'i. Sometimes we get busy when we eat and then we forget how much we have eaten. The late Allamah was determined to put in his plate at the beginning of each meal exactly what he had wanted to eat, and then not touch anything else.

There are many hadiths on the merits of fasting or eating little. For example, in his well-known advice to 'al-Unwān al-Basri, Imam Sadiq (a) said:

أَمَّا اللَّوَاتِى فِى الرِّيَاضَةِ فَإِيَّاكَ أَنْ تَأْكُلَ مَا لاتَشْتَهِيهِ فَإِنَّهُ يُورِثُ الْحَمَاقَةَ وَ الْبَلَهَ وَ لاتَأْكُلْ إِلا عِنْدَ الْجُوعِ وَ إِذَا أَكَلْتَ فَكُلْ حَلالا وَ سَمِّ اللَّهَ وَ اذْكُرْ حَدِيثَ الرَّسُولِ (ص) مَا مَلأَ آدَمِىٌّ وِعَاءً شَرّاً مِنْ بَطْنِهِ فَإِنْ كَانَ وَ لابُدَّ فَثُلُثٌ لِطَعَامِهِ وَ ثُلُثٌ لِشَرَابِهِ وَ ثُلُثٌ لِنَفَسِهِ

As for the three pieces of advice on self-discipline: firstly do not eat that which you have no appetite for, for this brings about idiocy and stupidity. Secondly do not eat unless you are hungry. And thirdly when you do eat, eat only that which is lawful (halāl) and begin in the Name of Allah, and remember the tradition of the Prophet (s): "Man has never filled any vessel worse than his own stomach". So if you must fill, then allow one third of it for food, another third for drink, and keep the last third for air.[1]

---

[1] *Bihar al-Anwar*, vol. 1, p. 226.

3. Not to sleep too much

This is especially important so that we do not waste our time and lose the golden opportunity of performing night prayers. Excessive comfort of the body is poisonous for the spirit. We need just the right amount of food and rest in order to have a healthy body because our body must be healthy to serve us.[1] But more than is necessary will be harmful for both our body and our spirit. Allah (swt) has created our body in such a way that when we look after our body we also end up looking after our spirit. We do not need to damage our body to become a pious person. If we eat too much we damage both our body and our spirit. If we sleep too much, do not take exercise and follow an inactive life-style, we will damage our body and our spirit. So it is very important not to sleep too much. In the Glorious Qur'an, Allah (swt) praises believers by saying:

إِنَّ الْمُتَّقِينَ فِي جَنَّاتٍ وَ عُيُونٍ ءَاخِذِينَ مَا ءَاتَهُمْ رَبُّهُمْ إِنَّهُمْ كَانُواْ قَبْلَ ذَالِكَ مُحْسِنِينَ كَانُواْ قَلِيلا مِّنَ اللَّيْلِ مَا يَهْجَعُونَ وَ بِالأَسْحَارِ هُمْ يَسْتَغْفِرُونَ وَ فِي أَمْوَالِهِمْ حَقٌّ لِّلسَّائِلِ وَ الْمَحْرُومِ

Indeed the Allah (swt) wary will be amid gardens and springs, receiving what their Lord has given them, for they had been virtuous aforetime. They used to sleep a little

---

[1] We can actually transform our eating and resting into acts of worship by making a good intention. For example, I can eat with the intention of becoming strong to serve Allah (swt) and therefore my eating or even preparation of the food becomes an act of worship, for which I will be rewarded.

during the night, and at dawn they would plead for forgiveness, and there was a share in their wealth for the beggar and the deprived. (51:15-19)

There are some people who do not sleep very much but the problem is that they do not know when it is the correct time to sleep. So they sleep at the time of the day which is best for worship and they are awake during the time which is least beneficial. For example, sometimes we sleep very late, after midnight, around 2 or 3am and then at the best time of the day for worship and contemplation we are un-conscious. The part of the day which is most important is the time before dawn and after dawn till sun rises. Whoever has achieved something, it is because they have appreciated this time. Allamah Tabātabā'i says that in the early days of his arrival in Najaf, his teacher, the late Ayatollah Sayyid Ali Qādi said to him: "If you want the *dunya* (this world), do *tahajjud* (night prayer); if you want the *akhira* (the hereafter), again do *tahajjud*".

4. To have private time to contemplate

We need some time to be alone, either during the day or more probably at night. It is good to promise ourselves that for at least ten or fifteen minutes each day we will just sit alone, for example on our prayer mat or in the garden, and think. This is enough to begin with. In time you will appreciate these private moments, such that you will wish your whole day to be spent in this way. This will lead to your life becoming stable, as investing this time creates a private space in your heart. In this way you can be active in society, and at the same time have an inner-peace and clear vision of your actions, as if you were alone. This can happen if you spend some time physically alone. When you gain control over the soul, you can be socialising, working, etc., and still maintain control over your actions, and have remembrance of Allah (swt).

But what should we think about during this private time?

We should think about divine attributes and actions. We should think about the things that we have done, about the things that we were supposed to do but did not and about the condition of our soul. We should decide if we are making any progress or not. If we have done something right then we should thank Allah (swt) for that. If we have done something wrong then we should try to remedy it. If we are not strong enough then we should fix some penalty on ourselves.

Sometimes people ask what they should do when they know that something is wrong and do not want to do it but they do it again and again anyway. For example, some people say that they do not have control over their anger and ask what they should do about this. They say that they are angry due to a psychological problem which they can do nothing about and that is out of their control. However, we should understand that Allah (swt) has given self-control to all of us, but the problem is that we ourselves may not exercise this power. There is an interesting story about this.

Once there was a person who had been newly employed in an office. On his first day at the office he told his new colleagues that he wanted to explain something to them straightaway so that in the future they would not feel upset or offended. He told them that unfortunately he was an angry person and that when he became angry he might shout at them, insult them or say something bad to them but that they should not feel upset or angry about it. One person who was listening to this was very clever. He thanked the new employee for saying this and told him that it was good that he had mentioned it. He said that now the new employee had been honest with them, he too would be honest with him. He said that he was also an angry person and that if anyone said something bad to him he had the habit of throwing whatever was within reach at the face of that person and so he was glad that the new employee had mentioned this. After this the new employee never became angry, he was always careful and watched what he said. This shows we can have self-control if we really try.

Sometimes we are very angry and aggressive at home but at work we are very calm. Even if people say bad things to us, we keep our anger inside. So it is possible for us to have self-control but in reality we choose not to. What should we do about this?

One thing that we can do is to fix a penalty for ourselves. For example, we can decide that if we become angry then we will do something that is difficult for us. And we must keep this promise that we have made to ourselves. We could promise that if we become angry and say something wrong to our spouse, our children or our parents, then we will donate a certain amount of money to charity, or fast the next day or walk ten kilometres. It should be something difficult. We will then see that we gain strength because our soul makes some kind of calculation that although it enjoys being angry and aggressive, it will also lose out due to the penalty that is imposed afterwards. So our soul will behave itself. This is called. "*musharitah*". Musharitah means to put some kind of condition on ourselves and to fix a penalty for breaking it. On the other hand, we can reward ourselves if we do something good. For example, if we like sweets very much then we can tell ourselves that we will not eat sweets unless we get up for our night prayers. If we get up, then we can have sweets. Then we will find that our soul will help us in getting up for our prayers because it wants sweets. So this is a technique that can help us to strengthen our determination.

The only time that we can think about and plan these kinds of things is when we have some private time alone. If we are always busy we cannot think about such things. But if we spend fifteen or twenty minutes alone with ourselves then we can achieve all these things. It is hard to know why people are afraid of being alone. We can often notice this. We love ourselves so much but the most painful thing for us is to be left to ourselves. If we are put in a room and locked in for 24 hours to be alone with ourselves, even if we are told that we will have food and all other necessities but just that we will be all alone, we will ask why we are being confined, imprisoned and tortured. But what is wrong with this? We have not been shut in with a wild animal or a criminal. We have only been asked to be alone with ourselves. Why do we not want to be alone with ourselves? There must be some unhealthy issue behind this. Imam Sajjad (a) says:

$$ لَوْ مَاتَ مَنْ بَيْنَ الْمَشْرِقِ وَ الْمَغْرِبِ لَمَا اسْتَوْحَشْتُ بَعْدَ أَنْ يَكُونَ الْقُرْآنُ مَعِى. $$

If all the people of the east and west die and I am left alone with the Qur'an I will not feel lonely.[1]

But most people are so afraid of being alone that they constantly make themselves busy. And if no one else is around, they will switch on the television or mp3 player or radio to make some noise so that they feel that they are not alone. But this is very bad. Sometimes we must try to be alone, have some privacy, have some rest and relaxation and think about the things that are very important.

5. Constant remembrance of Allah (swt).

Forgetting Allah (swt) is the source for all spiritual problems and naturally remembrance of Allah (swt) is the cure. In the Du'a of Kumayl, we read:

$$ اللَّهُمَّ إِنِّى أَتَقَرَّبُ إِلَيْكَ بِذِكْرِكَ $$

My Lord! I seek approximation to You with Your remembrance... [1]

---

[1] *Bihar al-Anwar,* vol. 46, p. 107.

يَا مَنِ اسْمُهُ دَوَآءٌ وَ ذِكْرُهُ شِفَاءٌ

O the One whose Name is medicine and whose remembrance is cure.[2]

Thus, remembrance of Allah (swt) brings tranquillity and light into the heart:

الَّذِينَ ءَامَنُواْ وَ تَطْمَئِنُّ قُلُوبُهُم بِذِكْرِ اللَّهِ أَلا بِذِكْرِ اللَّهِ تَطْمَئِنُّ الْقُلُوب

Those who believe and whose hearts find tranquillity by the remembrance of Allah; now surely by Allah's remembrance hearts find tranquillity. (13:28)

Imam Ali (a) says:

إِنَّ اللَّهَ سُبْحَانَهُ وَ تَعَالَى جَعَلَ الذِّكْرَ جَلاءً لِلْقُلُوب

Certainly Allah, the Glorified, has made His remembrance the luminosity and shine of the hearts.[3]

Thus, it becomes clear why so much emphasis has been put on the remembrance of Allah (swt). The Qur'an says:

وَ اذْكُر رَّبَّكَ كَثِيراً وَ سَبِّحْ بِالْعَشِيِّ وَ الابْكَار

Remember your Lord much and glorify Him in the evening and the morning. (3:41)

---

[1] *Iqbal al-a'mal*, vol. 2, p. 707.
[2] Ibid. p. 709.
[3] *Nahj al-Balaghah*, p. 342.

وَ اذْكُرِ اسْمَ رَبِّكَ وَ تَبَتَّلْ إِلَيْهِ تَبْتِيلا

*And remember the name of your Lord and devote yourself to
Him with exclusive devotion.* (73:8)

وَ اذْكُر رَّبَّكَ فِى نَفْسِكَ تَضَرُّعًا وَ خِيفَةً وَ دُونَ الْجَهْرِ مِنَ الْقَوْلِ بِالْغُدُوِّ
وَ الْآصَالِ وَ لاتَكُن مِّنَ الْغَافِلِين

*And remember your Lord within your heart beseechingly
and reverentially, without being loud, morning and evening,
and do not be among the heedless.* (7:205)

In Islam, everything has a limit even fasting and hajj. The only
exception is the remembrance of Allah (swt) which is always and
under all circumstances good and needed.[1] Ahmad b. Fahd Hilli
narrates from the Holy Prophet (s), that he said:

اعْلَمُوا أَنَّ خَيْرَ أَعْمَالِكُمْ وَ أَزْكَاهَا وَ أَرْفَعَهَا فِى دَرَجَاتِكُمْ وَ خَيْرَ مَا
طَلَعَتْ عَلَيْهِ الشَّمْسُ ذِكْرُ اللَّهِ سُبْحَانَهُ فَإِنَّهُ أَخْبَرَ عَنْ نَفْسِهِ فَقَالَ آنَا
جَلِيسُ مَنْ ذَكَرَنِى وَ قَالَ سُبْحَانَهُ فَاذْكُرُونِى أَذْكُرْكُمْ بِنِعْمَتِى وَ اذْكُرُونِى
بِالطَّاعَةِ وَ الْعِبَادَةِ أَذْكُرْكُمْ بِالنِّعَمِ وَ الْإِحْسَانِ وَ الرَّحْمَةِ وَ الرِّضْوَان

*Be informed that the best of your acts near Allah (swt), and
the purest and highest of them in degree, and the best thing
upon which the sun has shone is the remembrance of Allah*

---

[1] *Al-Kafi*, vol. 2, p. 498. The original text is as follows:

«مَا مِنْ شَىْءٍ إِلا وَ لَهُ حَدٌّ يَنْتَهِى إِلَيْهِ إِلا الذِّكْرُ فَلَيْسَ لَهُ حَدٌّ يَنْتَهِى إِلَيْهِ»

Almighty. Verily he has informed you saying: "I am the companion of him who remembers Me.[1]

Constant remembrance of Allah (swt) is both difficult and not difficult to do. It is not difficult because it does not cost us anything, we do not need to pay for it or go to a special place or do any physical exercise. So it should be very easy, as are all the other practices mentioned above, none of which costs us anything and so they are very cost effective methods when we consider the results which they can produce. However, it is also very difficult to do because our soul always tries to indulge itself, to do what it wants and does not want to be disciplined. But if we discipline our soul then things become easy.

Remembrance of Allah (swt) is healing. The Names of Allah (swt) are medicine and if we take this medicine in order to remember Allah (swt) then we will be healed, but if we constantly repeat invocations like '*Allahu Akbar*' again and again but do not remember Allah (swt)then we are just keeping our mouths busy with repetitions and this is not proper remembrance of Allah (swt). However if we use the Names of Allah (swt) to remember Him then this is the healing. It is very easy to do this. For example, we can be driving or walking or doing whatever we have to do and still be remembering Allah (swt). The Qur'an speaks of the people who do not forget Allah (swt) even when they are involved in business and commerce. They always remember Allah

---

[1] *'Uddat al-Da'i*, p. 253.

(swt). We may be cooking or washing, teaching or studying, but at the same time we must remember Allah (swt). So we need to remember Allah (swt) and these invocations are means to help us to keep our concentration. All the different dhikrs (like *Allahu Akbar*, *Alhamdullillah* and *Subhanallah*) are medicines but we must take these medicines correctly by remembering Allah (swt), by trying to get close to that Attribute of Allah (swt) which we are mentioning and then we will feel that we are closer to Allah (swt).

So this is the way in which we should remember Allah (swt) and if we taste the sweetness and beauty of true remembrance of Allah (swt) then we will never be pleased with anything else. We need to rid ourselves of all the bad things inside us and then we will start to really enjoy remembrance of Allah (swt).

If we spend some private time alone then we can start to learn how to remember Allah (swt) during that private time and then expand this to the rest of our lives. In the beginning we may only remember Allah (swt) when we are on our prayer mat. But gradually we can try to remember Allah (swt) throughout the day. And then remembrance of Allah (swt) becomes constant.

A practical suggestion to incorporate these attitudes into your life

As we saw above, there are five important things that we need to observe: not to speak too much, not to eat too much, not to sleep too much, to have private time for contemplation (not to mix with people too much or keep ourselves too busy) and to remember Allah (s.w.t) constantly. These are five very easy things to do which do not cost anything. They are five powerful vitamins for our spiritual health and growth. If one maintains them for several weeks he will certainly start feeling the difference and will see the results.

One practical step is to keep a notebook and set out some objectives for yourself each day. Give a mark to yourself for each category. Whenever needed also make some comments. Then on a regular basis review your comments and evaluate your progress. Do this every day and compare your actions with the objectives. If all the actions are good, thank Allah (swt) and continue. If some areas are bad, try and improve. For the first few weeks, do not take any chances by delaying this process for any reason. Complete the chart in all circumstances. This brings discipline into to your life. If you feel as though you are achieving, you will feel more determined. If you feel there are areas in which you cannot improve, even though you try to, fix a penalty for yourself. For example, if I notice that last week I kept getting angry, I should find an action which I find difficult to do, such as housework; then set myself the penalty: for example I might say "if I get angry again, I will do all the housework for 2 days". By the time I have undertaken the penalty a few times, I will learn to think before I get angry, and stop myself. In the same way, to give an incentive for good actions, you can set yourself a reward. In this way you can increase your determination. Allah's (swt) help will always be there for those who strive in Him:

وَ الَّذِينَ جَاهَدُواْ فِينَا لَنَهْدِيَنَّهُمْ سُبُلَنَا وَ إِنَّ اللَّهَ لَمَعَ الْمُحْسِنِينَ

*As for those who strive in Us, We shall surely guide them
in Our ways, and Allah is indeed with the virtuous.* (29:69)

It is also very helpful to have close friends who have the same
inclinations, with whom you can discuss your progress and
problems. In this way, you can also advise each other. The
Qur'an says:

إِنَّ الانسَانَ لَفِى خُسْرٍ إِلا الَّذِينَ ءَامَنُواْ وَ عَمِلُواْ الصَّالِحَاتِ وَ تَوَاصَوْاْ
بِالْحَقّ وَ تَوَاصَوْاْ بِالصَّبر

*Most surely man is in loss. Except those who believe and do
good, and enjoin on each other truth, and enjoin on each
other patience.* (103: 2-3)

Conclusion

In this article, we have reviewed the various practical ways in
which we can perform self-building. By speaking little, eating
little, sleeping little, keeping private time, and remembering Allah
(swt), we can really begin to achieve closeness to Allah (swt)
through purification of the soul. The techniques discussed above
are neither strenuous nor costly; rather, they require patience and
determination. We pray that Allah (swt) grants this to us so that
we may gain the true reward: proximity to Him (swt). May Allah
(swt) help us *all!*

Outcomes of the Spiritual Journey[1]

It is clear that the ultimate aim of the spiritual journey is to get as close to Allah (swt) as possible. However, the notion of closeness (qurb) to Allah (swt) may appear to some as abstract, especially for those who are not trained in philosophy. This essay attempts to shed light on the notion of closeness to Allah (swt) by describing what happens to those who are undergoing the spiritual journey towards Him. All the ideas mentioned henceforth are derived from the Qur'an and Sunnah and therefore are hoped to be welcomed by all Muslims from different schools of Islam. Reflection on these outcomes can encourage everyone to embark on this journey and, if they have already done so, to continue following this luminous path. It can also serve as a test for the wayfarers to assess how much progress they have made. Insha-Allah, in an upcoming issue, we will study the notion of closeness to Allah (swt) as a subject on its own and explain what it means to become close to Allah (swt) (*qarib*) and who the *muqarrabin* (the people that are brought even closer) are.

---

[1] This essay is revised version of a similar title published in the *Message of Thaqalayn*, vol. 11, no. 3.

Outcomes of the spiritual journey

1. Complete support: One of the outcomes of living a life of piety and having a pure and pious heart is that we will be given complete support by Allah (swt). He will listen to us, will give us what we want, and will be our ears, eyes and hands. In the well-known divine saying (*hadith-i qudsi*) of *qurb-i nawāfil*, we read:

مَا تَقَرَّبَ إِلَيَّ عَبْدٌ بِشَيْءٍ أَحَبَّ إِلَيَّ مِمَّا افْتَرَضْتُ عَلَيْهِ وَ إِنَّهُ لَيَتَقَرَّبُ
إِلَيَّ بِالنَّافِلَةِ حَتَّى أُحِبَّهُ فَإِذَا أَحْبَبْتُهُ كُنْتُ سَمْعَهُ الَّذِى يَسْمَعُ بِهِ وَ بَصَرَهُ
الَّذِى يُبْصِرُ بِهِ وَ لِسَانَهُ الَّذِى يَنْطِقُ بِهِ وَ يَدَهُ الَّتِى يَبْطِشُ بِهَا إِنْ دَعَانِى
أَجَبْتُهُ وَ إِنْ سَأَلَنِى أَعْطَيْتُهُ

None of My servants can seek proximity to Me by that which is dearer to Me than things that I have made obligatory on him. Then, with the performance of nawāfil (the recommended acts), he continuously attains proximity to Me, so that I love him. When I love him, I will be the ear with which he hears, the eyes with which he sees, and the hand with which he strikes. If he calls Me, I will answer his call, and if he makes a request, I will grant it.[1]

2. Perfect knowledge: There are many hadiths which indicate that one of the results of having attained spiritual nearness to Allah (swt)is to be endowed with great knowledge of the realities of the world, including many mysteries that can never be known through ordinary methods of learning and teaching. On the topic

---

[1] *Al-Kāfi*, vol. 2, pp. 352 & 353.

of the servant who has attained proximity to Allah (swt), Prophet Muhammad (s) reports Allah (swt) as saying:

فَإِذَا أَحَبَّنِى أَحْبَبْتُهُ وَ أَفْتَحُ عَيْنَ قَلْبِهِ إِلَى جَلَالِى وَ لَاأُخْفِى عَلَيْهِ خَاصَّةَ خَلْقِى وَ أُنَاجِيهِ فِى ظُلَمِ اللَّيْلِ وَ نُورِ النَّهَارِ حَتَّى يَنْقَطِعَ حَدِيثُهُ مَعَ الْمَخْلُوقِينَ وَ مُجَالَسَتُهُ مَعَهُمْ وَ أُسْمِعُهُ كَلَامِى وَ كَلَامَ مَلَائِكَتِى وَ أُعَرِّفُهُ السِّرَّ الَّذِى سَتَرْتُهُ عَنْ خَلْقِى

I will love him when he loves Me and I will make him loved by My creation, and I will open up his inward eyes to My glory and grandeur, and I will not hide from him [the knowledge of] the select of My creation. So in the darkness of night and in the light of day, I will tell him secrets, so that his conversations with creatures and with his companions will be cut off. I will make him hear My words and the words of My angels and I will reveal to him the secret I have hidden from My creation.[1]

3. Exclusive devotion to Allah (swt): To be cut off from everything other than Allah (swt) (*tabattul or inqita*) means to be free from reliance on anything other than Allah (swt), and to see everything as His sign and as a manifestation of His power and grace. The true servants of Allah (swt) live within society while remaining totally mindful of Allah (swt), and they remember Him continuously. The Qur'an praises a group of people "whom neither business nor trading distract from remembering Allah

---

[1] *Bihār al-Anwār*, vol. 74, pp. 28 & 29.

(swt), keeping up prayer, and giving alms".[1] In the well-known Whisper of Sha'bān (al-Mmunajāt al-Sha'bāniyyah), Imam Ali (a) and other members of the household of the Prophet (s) called upon Allah (swt), saying:

إِلَهِي هَبْ لِي كَمَالَ الِانْقِطَاعِ إِلَيْكَ وَ أَنِرْ أَبْصَارَ قُلُوبِنَا بِضِيَاءِ نَظَرِهَا
إِلَيْكَ حَتَّى تَخْرِقَ أَبْصَارُ الْقُلُوبِ حُجُبَ النُّورِ فَتَصِلَ إِلَى مَعْدِنِ الْعَظَمَةِ
وَ تَصِيرَ أَرْوَاحُنَا مُعَلَّقَةً بِعِزِّ قُدْسِكَ

*My Allah (swt)! Make me completely cut off from all else
but You, and enlighten the vision of our hearts with the
radiance of looking at You, until the vision of our hearts
penetrates the veils of light and reaches the Source of
Grandeur and set our spirit to be suspended at the glory of
Your sanctity.*[2]

In this supplication, the Imam (a) is asking Allah (swt) to enable him to be related only to Him and to be detached from anything that stops us from being in His presence.

Unfortunately there are many actions that can hinder our devotion, which could be apparently good or bad. Of course, bad actions and sins can keep us away from Allah's remembrance, but good actions can also become corrupted, for example, by arrogance and pride. Therefore, we should not let anything

---

[1] Chapter 24 verse 37. The Arabic text is as follows:
«رِجَالٌ لَاتُلْهِيهِمْ تِجَارَةٌ وَ لَا بَيْعٌ عَن ذِكْرِ اللَّهِ وَ إِقَامِ الصَّلَوةِ وَ إِيتَاءِ الزَّكَوةِ ...»
[2] *Iqbal al-a'mal*, vol. 2, p. 687.

become a barrier or a veil between us and Allah (swt), the Source of Light and Grandeur, whether it be our sins and attachment to the material life or our good actions and characteristics. If we are not careful, even good actions and qualities can preoccupy our mind and heart, therefore diverting our attention away from Allah (swt). It is interesting that Imam Ali (a) asks to "penetrate the veils of light." According to Ayatollah Khomeini, "the veils of light" refers to those veils which are in and of themselves light, but prevent us from beholding the main light, which is Allah (swt). This is why knowledge, which is so highly regarded in Islam and everyone is required to seek it, can become "the greatest veil" (*al-hijāb al-akbar*). It is like someone who has a pair of glasses to help him read, but instead of using it to read, he simply holds it in his hand, enjoys looking at it, or plays with it. Of course, the knowledge which comes after the purification of one's soul is different. According to hadiths, this type of knowledge is a light that Allah (swt) projects into the heart of the one with whom He is pleased.[1] The following story, narrated in the biography of Allamah Sayyid Mohammad Husayn Tabataba'i, relates to this point. Once Allamah was given an instruction for a specific practice by his spiritual teacher, Ayatollah Sayyid Ali Qādi Tabataba'i, and was advised that "when you are doing this special practice you may start seeing angels, but you should continue with your practice and should not be distracted." Once Allamah

---

[1] *Misbah al- Shari'ah*, p. 1. The original text is as follows:

«قَالَ الصَّادِقُ (ع): ... الْعِلْمُ نُورٌ يَقْذِفُهُ اللَّهُ فِى قَلْبِ مَنْ يَشَاءُ»

was conducting his worship and he saw an angel coming towards him. He immediately remembered what his teacher had told him and continued worshipping. Then the angel went around him as if he wanted to start a conversation with Allamah, but he did not pay any attention, so the angel sadly left him. Allamah remarked that he would never forget the sadness of that angel, but this is the way a true servant devotes himself to His Lord. We should not let anything get in the way of our focused devotion.

4. Entrance into the realm of light.

The above hadiths and many others refer to the fact that one of the results of progress on the spiritual journey is the elimination of darkness and entrance into the realm of light. The realm of light is a reality mentioned in the Qur'an and hadith:

اللَّهُ وَلِيُّ الَّذِينَ ءَامَنُواْ يُخْرِجُهُم مِّنَ الظُّلُمَاتِ إِلَى النُّور

Allah is the guardian of those who believe. He brings them out of the darkness into the light (2:257)

يَهْدِى بِهِ اللَّهُ مَنِ اتَّبَعَ رِضْوَانَهُ سُبُلَ السَّلَمِ وَ يُخْرِجُهُم مِّنَ الظُّلُمَاتِ إِلَى النُّورِ بِإِذْنِهِ وَ يَهْدِيهِمْ إِلَى صِرَاطٍ مُّسْتَقِيم

With it Allah guides him who will follow His pleasure into the ways of safety and brings them out of utter darkness into light by His will and guides them to the right path. (5:16)

Light is also requested in many supplications, such as in the prayer which should be recited after the *Ziyarah* of *Aal-i Yāsin*:

اللَّهُمَّ إِنِّى أَسْأَلُكَ أَنْ تُصَلِّىَ عَلَى مُحَمَّدٍ نَبِيِّ رَحْمَتِكَ وَ كَلِمَةِ نُورِكَ وَ
أَنْ تَمْلأَ قَلْبِى نُورَ الْيَقِينِ وَ صَدْرِى نُورَ الإِيمَانِ وَ فِكْرِى نُورَ النِّيَّاتِ وَ
عَزْمِى نُورَ الْعِلْمِ وَ قُوَّتِى نُورَ الْعَمَلِ وَ لِسَانِى نُورَ الصِّدْقِ وَ دِينِى نُورَ
الْبَصَائِرِ مِنْ عِنْدِكَ وَ بَصَرِى نُورَ الضِّيَاءِ وَ سَمْعِى نُورَ الْحِكْمَةِ وَ مَوَدَّتِى
نُورَ الْمُوَالاةِ لِمُحَمَّدٍ وَ آلِهِ عَلَيْهِمُ السَّلامُ حَتَّى أَلْقَاكَ وَ قَدْ وَفَيْتُ بِعَهْدِكَ
وَ مِيثَاقِكَ فَتَغَشِّيَنِى رَحْمَتَكَ يَا وَلِىُّ يَا حَمِيدُ

*O Allah, surely I ask You to send blessings upon
Muhammad (s), the prophet of Your mercy and the
word of Your light.*

*And fill my heart with the light of certainty
And my chest with light of faith.*

And my thinking with the light of intentions.

And my determination with the light of knowledge.

And my power with the light of action.

And my tongue with the light of truthfulness.

And my religion with the light of understanding from You.

And my vision with brightness.

And my hearing with the light of wisdom.

*And my love with the light of friendship for Muhammad (s)
and his progeny. Peace be upon (all of) them!*

*Until I meet You, while certainly I discharged Your promise
and Your covenant. So You cover me with Your mercy, O
Master! O Praiseworthy.*[1]

In the realm of light, everything is clear and the true reality of
everything is known. One of the main challenges we face is to

---

[1] *Bihar al-Anwar*, vol. 53, p.172.

understand everything the way it really is, and to treat each thing appropriately.

5. Immense love for Allah (swt): One of the strongest ways to strengthen our relationship with Allah (swt) is through love for Him. Once one has tasted this love, there is no other substitute. The Imams (a) were consumed with love for Allah (swt). Imam Ali b. Husayn (a) says:

غُلَّتِى لاَيُرَدُّهَا إِلا وَصْلُكَ وَ لَوْعَتِى لاَيُطْفِيهَا إِلا لِقَاوُكَ وَ شَوْقِى إِلَيْكَ لاَيَبُلُّهُ إِلا النَّظَرُ إِلَى وَجْهِكَ وَ قَرَارِى لا يَقِرُّ دُونَ دُنُوِّى مِنْكَ

Nothing will cool my burning thirst but reaching You, quench my ardour but meeting You, damp my yearning but gazing upon Your face, settle my settling place without closeness to you.[1]

The mystic is not the one who just loves Allah (swt); rather he is the one who loves Allah (swt) alone, because his love or dislike for anything else is only for the sake of Allah (swt). He wills and desires only what his Beloved wills and desires. He has no will or desire other than His. The mystic's love for Allah (swt) permeates his love for anything else.[2] Imam Sadiq (a) says:

الْقَلْبُ السَّلِيمُ الَّذِى يَلْقَى رَبَّهُ وَ لَيْسَ فِيهِ أَحَدٌ سِوَاه

---

[1] *The Psalms of Islam*, pp. 251 & 252.
[2] For a detailed account of love, see *Love in Christianity and Islam* (2005, 2nd edition) by Mahnaz Heydarpoor.

The pure heart is the one that meets the Lord while it is free from anyone else.[1]

6. Witnessing Allah (swt) in everything: The real mystic is the one who witnesses Allah (swt) in everything. Allah (swt) constantly shows Himself to us in different ways, and if our hearts are pure, we can witness Allah (swt) through all things. In *Duā of 'Arafah*, Imam Husayn (a) says:

اِلهى عَلِمْتُ بِاخْتِلافِ الْأثَارِ وَتَنَقُّلاتِ الْأطْوارِ اَنَّ مُرادَكَ مِنّى اَنْ تَتَعَرَّفَ اِلَىَّ فى كُلِّشَىْءٍ حَتّى لا اَجْهَلَكَ فى شَىْءٍ

O my Allah (swt)! Through the variety of Your signs (in the world of being) and the changes in states and conditions, I realised that the purpose is to make Yourself known to me in everything, so that I would not ignore You in anything.[2]

Imam Ali (a) says:

ما رأيت شيئًا الا و قد رأيت الله قبله و بعده و معه و فيه

I saw nothing except that I saw Allah (swt) before it, with it, and after it.[3]

It is obvious that the vision in question, for Allah (swt), the Almighty, is infinitely exalted beyond the range of the physical

---

[1] *Al-Kāfi*, vol. 2, p. 16.

[2] *Bihār al-Anwār*, vol. 95, p. 225.

[3] *al-Hikmat al-Mute'ahia fi al-Asfār al-Arba'ah,* vol. 1, p. 117.

eye. Allah (swt) cannot be seen by the physical eye, neither in this world nor in the hereafter.

Being busy usually means that we forget Allah (swt) and become consumed with our dealings. However, for Imam Ali (a), it meant that he remembered Allah (swt) all the time: before, during and after each thing; as Allah (swt) is the Creator, Preserver, and the one who will remain after all things.

One who has reached a high stage in the spiritual journey will find Allah (swt) in everything. For example, even if someone tells us something bad or our enemy tells us something, we can still manage to find a good message inside that which only we are able to de-code and understand. Other people may listen to the same thing but they do not get any message from it. However, we will understand the message from Allah (swt) even in the words of our enemy.

7. Internal peace: Whenever a man gets close to Allah (swt), all other things appear light and small to him. He feels that he is under Allah's protection, and nothing can harm him. He understands that he does not suffer any pain or difficulty except that they are to his own benefit, and that he will be rewarded by Allah (swt) "without measure".[1]

---

[1] Chapter 39 verse 10. The Arabic text is as follows:

«إِنَّمَا يُوَفَّى الصَّابِرُونَ أَجْرَهُم بِغَيْرِ حِسَابٍ»

There are many people in the world who have comfortable lives, but they suffer from a lack of peace and tranquillity, to the extent that some of them resort to alcoholic drinks or narcotic drugs to decrease their spiritual pain and self-consciousness. However, nothing short of reaching Allah (swt) can satisfy human beings. The Qur'an says:

ألا بِذِكْرِ اللَّهِ تَطْمَئِنُّ الْقُلُوب

Surely! With the remembrance of Allah (swt) hearts come to rest. (13:28)

One reason why nothing can disturb people who are mindful of Allah (swt) is that they are not afraid of losing anything. Everything becomes easy for them, since they have appreciated Allah's (swt) greatness, nothing else is important in their view. For example, if you are on a beach next to the ocean, you would not pay any attention to a small glass of water. Describing the pious (*al-muttaqin*), Imam Ali (a) says:

عَظُمَ الْخَالِقُ فِى أَنْفُسِهِمْ فَصَغُرَ ما دُونَهُ فِى أَعْيُنِهِمْ

The greatness of the Creator is seated in their hearts and so everything else appears small in their eyes.[1]

Conclusion

The outcomes of the spiritual journey are too many to describe in this short essay. The journey rewards those who travel on its path

---

[1] *Nahj al-Balāghah*, p. 303.

with exclusive devotion, entrance into the realm of light, immense love for Allah (swt), being able to witness Allah (swt) in everything, and internal peace. Once we take a step towards Allah (swt), He will reward us with these invaluable blessings, which will make it easier for us to travel farther.

The Supreme Light and Created Lights:
A Qur'anic Perspective[1]

Of the most important names Allah (swt) uses to describe
Himself in the Qur'an is that of light (*noor*). Allah (swt) Himself
is the supreme Light and all that He created are also lights. Using
the Qur'an and Islamic traditions, this article addresses some of
the major aspects of the concept of light. Light is one of Allah's
qualities, and every being in the universe is endowed with it.
Moreover, the amount of light all creatures hold depends on the
capacity of their existence; some beings have a fixed amount of
light, while rational beings with free will, that is, human beings
and jinn, can increase their light with faith and good deeds, or
decrease it with disbelief and transgression.

Introduction

Different names and notions are used by people to refer to Allah
(swt), though without a doubt the most important names are
those used by Allah (swt) Himself. Among the notions used in
reference to Allah (swt) in the Holy Qur'an is that of light (*noor*).

---

[1] This essay is a revised version of a similar title published in the *Message of
Thaqalayn*, vol. 14, no. 4.

It has the advantage in that most people generally comprehend and like this concept. Moreover, many express interest in it and long to escape its opposite, which is darkness. It can be understood from the Qur'an and Islamic traditions that this concept has a range spanning the entire universal existence and is capable of being the basis for a theological and systematic account of the entire world. In this article, we will attempt to address some of the major aspects of this account.

Light as one of Allah's qualities

In various languages and religious cultures, the use of the word light in reference to Allah (swt) is not uncommon, and many passages in the Qur'an and hadith affirm the appropriateness of its usage. The Qur'an states:

اللَّهُ نُورُ السَّمَاوَاتِ وَ الأَرْضِ مَثَلُ نُورِهِ كَمِشْكَوةٍ فِيهَا مِصْبَاحٌ الْمِصْبَاحُ فِى زُجَاجَةٍ الزُّجَاجَةُ كَأَنَّهَا كَوْكَبٌ دُرِّيٌّ يُوقَدُ مِن شَجَرَةٍ مُّبَارَكَةٍ زَيْتُونَةٍ لاشَرْقِيَّةٍ وَ لاغَرْبِيَّةٍ

Allah (swt) is the Light of the heavens and the earth. The parable of His Light is a niche wherein is a lamp - the lamp is in a glass, the glass as it were a glittering star - lit from a blessed olive tree, neither eastern nor western... (24:35)

In this verse, known as Ayat al-Noor (the 'Verse of Light') in chapter *Noor,* Allah (swt) describes himself as the Light of the heavens and the earth; Allah (swt) is Light, the heavens and the earth have light, and the light of the heavens and the earth stem from Allah (swt). There are additional verses that use the term "Allah's light;" however, upon reflection, it becomes clear that they are not about the light which is Allah (swt) Himself. Rather, what is meant is that light that is from Allah (swt):

يُرِيدُونَ أَن يُطْفِؤُواْ نُورَ اللَّهِ بِأَفْوَاهِهِمْ وَ يَأْبَى اللَّهُ إِلا أَن يُتِمَّ نُورَهُ وَ لَوْ كَرِهَ الْكَفِرُونَ

They desire to put out the light of Allah (swt) with their mouths, but Allah (swt) is intent on perfecting His light though the faithless should be averse. (9:32)

يُرِيدُونَ لِيُطْفِؤُواْ نُورَ اللَّهِ بِأَفْوَاهِهِمْ وَ اللَّهُ مُتِمُّ نُورِهِ وَ لَوْ كَرِهَ الْكَافِرُونَ

They desire to put out the light of Allah (swt) with their mouths, but Allah (swt) shall perfect His light though the faithless should be averse. (61:8)

Thus, the 'light' that the opponents of truth and virtues set out to destroy is light that is from Allah (swt), and not the light of Allah (swt) himself. This light is Allah's creation and can be increased. But if 'light' were to indicate the light which is Allah (swt) Himself, its completion would have no meaning, since Allah (swt) is the Absolute light.

In the du'a (supplication) of Jawshan Kabeer, we read:

يَا نُورَ النُّورِ يَا مُنَوِّرَ النُّورِ يَا خَالِقَ النُّورِ يَا مُدَبِّرَ النُّورِ يَا مُقَدِّرَ النُّورِ يَا نُورَ كُلِّ نُورٍ يَا نُورًا قَبْلَ كُلِّ نُورٍ يَا نُورًا بَعْدَ كُلِّ نُورٍ يَا نُورًا فَوْقَ كُلِّ نُورٍ يَا نُورًا لَيْسَ كَمِثْلِهِ نُورٌ

O Light of lights, O Illuminator of light, O Creator of light, O Planner of light, O Estimator of light, O Light of all lights, O Light that precedes in existence every light, O Light that will survive all lights, O Light that is above every light, O Light like of which there is no light. (Article 47)[1]

We also read in Du‘a ‘Ahd:

اللَّهُمَّ رَبَّ النُّورِ الْعَظِيمِ وَ رَبَّ الْكُرْسِيِّ الرَّفِيعِ وَ رَبَّ الْبَحْرِ الْمَسْجُورِ وَ مُنْزِلَ التَّوْرَاةِ وَ الإِنْجِيلِ وَ الزَّبُورِ وَ رَبَّ الظِّلِّ وَ الْحَرُورِ وَ مُنْزِلَ الْقُرْآنِ الْعَظِيمِ وَ رَبَّ الْمَلَائِكَةِ الْمُقَرَّبِينَ وَ الأَنْبِيَاءِ [وَ] الْمُرْسَلِينَ اللَّهُمَّ إِنِّي أَسْأَلُكَ بِوَجْهِكَ الْكَرِيمِ وَ بِنُورِ وَجْهِكَ الْمُنِيرِ وَ مُلْكِكَ الْقَدِيمِ يَا حَيُّ يَا قَيُّومُ أَسْأَلُكَ بِاسْمِكَ الَّذِى أَشْرَقَتْ بِهِ السَّمَاوَاتُ وَ الأَرَضُونَ وَ بِاسْمِكَ الَّذِى يَصْلَحُ بِهِ الأَوَّلُونَ وَ الآخِرُونَ

O Allah! Lord of the Great Light, Lord of the Elevated Throne, Lord of the tumultuous seas, and the revealer of the Tawrah, Injeel, and Zaboor, Lord of the shadows and the warmths, and the revealer of the Great Qur'an. Lord of the proximate angels and prophets and messengers. O Allah, I beseech thee, for the sake of Your Nobel Visage, and for the sake of Your Enlightening Visage, and Your ever existing kingdom. O Ever Living! O Controller! I beseech Thee in Your Name which lit the heavens and the earths; and in

---

[1] *Bihar al-Anwar*, vol. 91, p. 390.

Your Name, by which the ancient and the latter ones become upright.[1]

We also read in the Dua of Kumayl: "Oh Light, oh Holy [One]."[2]

Allah (swt) is a Light that is far from any defect. In other words, Allah (swt) is an absolute Light in which darkness has no way in. Indeed, darkness is the same as the limitation or defect of light, which can only be conceivable in created lights. This will be explained further below.

Every creature has light

As mentioned earlier, the heavens and the earth – which is for all of existence in the universe – are illuminated through Allah's light and are radiant.[3] Right now the heavens and the earth shine: "...I beseech Thee in Your Name which lit the heavens and the earths" (Du'a 'Ahd). Thus, the Qur'an's statement of the earth's radiance with Allah's light on the Day of Judgment does not indicate that there is an absence of light at present; rather, it means that on the Day of Judgment the earth's radiance will reveal itself and, without the help of sunlight, electricity, and the like, the earth will glow by means of a Allah (swt)-given light.

---

[1] Ibid. vol. 53, p. 95.

[2] *Iqbal al-a'mal*, vol. 2, p. 707. The original text is as follows:

«نُورُ يَا قُدُّوس»

[3] For example, see the verse 24:35 and the extracts from the du'as.

Referring to the fact that everything is made as a kind of light, the Qur'an says:

الْحَمْدُ لِلَّهِ الَّذِى خَلَقَ السَّمَاوَاتِ وَ الأَرْضَ وَ جَعَلَ الظُّلُمَاتِ وَ النُّورَ

ثُمَّ الَّذِينَ كَفَرُواْ بِرَبِّهِمْ يَعْدِلُون

All praise belongs to Allah Who created the heavens and the earth and made the darknesses and the light. Yet the faithless equate [others] with their Lord. (6:1)

The creation of the heavens and the earth, and the structure of the universal system based on light and darkness means that every being on this universe is endowed with light. This is a common trait shared by all beings, a trait derived from their Creator who is absolute Light. At the same time, the difference between created beings is also related to the fact that they are light. This is because non-light is equivalent to darkness, and darkness - like a shadow - is the absence of matter. This is in fact, according to philosophy, the same as gradation (tashkik) in which the differentiating factor is the same as the common factor. In other words, what all of creation have in common is the fact that they each have light, but they differ in their levels of its intensity.

A being with absolutely no light is inconceivable – there is no such thing as absolute darkness. Based on the premise that the Creator is absolute light, and that light is consequently attributed to Him, all beings possess some degree of light. Every being is a sign of the Divine and in this way is reflective of the Divine's light. If we perceive all beings from this point of view, we see them as having light, and since this serves as a sign of Allah (swt) and reminds us of Allah (swt), it will also be the source of our getting closer to Him. If someone or something brings darkness to our hearts and renders us heedless of Allah (swt), it is not because they are absolutely dark; rather it is because they divert our attention away from Allah (swt) by drawing our attention to themselves or anything independent from Allah (swt) or it is because we have not approached them properly.

In Du'a Kumayl we read, "And by the light of Your face, for which all things are illumined."[1]   When creations' attention is turned to Allah (swt), they illuminate, and if we see them from this angle, we will also be able to witness this illumination because they will also manifest as the "face" of Allah (swt), as said in the verse, "...*so whichever way you turn, there is the face of Allah.*"[2]

The amount of light creatures hold depends on the capacity of their existence

For most creatures, their capacity for light is not determined voluntarily and therefore, their light is incapable of escalation or decline.   Angels, who have high degrees of brightness, have a

---

[1] *Iqbal al-a'mal*, vol. 2, p. 707. The original text is as follows:

«وَ بِنُورِ وَجْهِكَ الَّذِى أَضَاءَ لَهُ كُلُّ شَىْءٍ»

[2] Chapter 2 verse 115. The Arabic text is as follows:

«فَأَيْنَمَا تُوَلُّوا فَثَمَّ وَجْهُ اللَّهِ»

fixed capacity: *"There is none among us but has a known place."*[1] This is true for angels as a whole [with respect to other beings] as well as individually [in relation to one another]. For example, no matter how hard angels try, they cannot reach the position of Adam, Allah's vicegerent. Likewise, Angel Michael cannot reach Angel Gabriel's position, nor can Angel Gabriel descend to Angel Michael's level.

Humans (and Jinn) on the other hand possess freedom of choice and, as a result, if they choose the right path, they can acquire more light; if they choose the wrong path, their light will subside. Therefore, there are three possible states for humans:

a. The inherent state in which humans naturally possess light and with it can ascend to high levels of nearness to Allah (swt). Every human is created pure: "Every child is born with a pure nature."[2] And every human is created in the best way: *"We certainly created man in the best of forms."*[3] They are also guided and it is through their own choice that they establish their future: *"Then We relegated him to the lowest of the low, except those who have faith and do righteous deeds. There will be an everlasting*

---

[1] Chapter 37 verse 164. The Arabic text is as follows:

«وَ مَا مِنَّا إِلا لَهُ مَقَامٌ مَّعْلُوم»

[2] *al-Kafi*, vol. 2, p. 13. The original text is as follows:

« كل مولود يولد على الفطره»

[3] Chapter 95 verse 4. The Arabic text is as follows:

«لَقَدْ خَلَقْنَا الانسَانَ فِى أَحْسَنِ تَقْوِيم»

reward for them".[1] Every human being has been given enough light to find his way towards Allah (swt) and perfection. Of course, based on different factors, humans may also possess different degrees of light from the beginning, as they may have different levels of intelligence. In any case, they all have immense brightness and encounter enough light to find the path and embark on it.

b. The state of acquired faith and purity that increases human brightness and can eventually make him Allah's vicegerent, allowing him to spread brightness among other creatures.

c. The state of acquired disbelief and impurity that decreases human brightness to the point where one becomes lower than an animal, or the lowest of the low (asfala safileen). We read in the Qur'an:

اللَّهُ وَلِيُّ الَّذِينَ ءَامَنُواْ يُخْرِجُهُم مِّنَ الظُّلُمَاتِ إِلَى النُّورِ وَ الَّذِينَ كَفَرُواْ أَوْلِيَاؤُهُمُ الطَّاغُوتُ يُخْرِجُونَهُم مِّنَ النُّورِ إِلَى الظُّلُمَاتِ أُوْلَئِكَ أَصْحَبُ النَّارِ هُمْ فِيهَا خَالِدُون

Allah (swt) is the Guardian of the faithful: He brings them out of darkness into light. As for the faithless, their patrons are the Rebels, who drive them out of light into darkness.

---

[1] Chapter 95 verses 5 & 6. The Arabic text is as follows:

«ثُمَّ رَدَدْنَاهُ أَسْفَلَ سَافِلِينَ إِلا الَّذِينَ ءَامَنُواْ وَ عَمِلُواْ الصَّالِحَاتِ فَلَهُمْ أَجْرٌ غَيْرُ مَمْنُون»

The Qur'an also says:

«إِنَّا هَدَيْنَاهُ السَّبِيلَ إِمَّا شَاكِرًا وَ إِمَّا كَفُورًا»

"Indeed We have guided him to the way, be he grateful or ungrateful." (76:3)

*They shall be the inmates of the Fire, and they shall remain
in it [forever].* (2:257)

This verse eloquently illustrates the above three points. Initially it
may appear as if there are four states: First, the state of darkness
before faith; Second, light that comes after faith; Third, the state
of light before disbelief; and Fourth, darkness after disbelief.
However, after contemplation, it becomes clear that the above
verse refers to the same three states mentioned above:

Considering that a) the states of faith and disbelief are acquired
and b) the state before faith and disbelief is the first innate and
natural state, a person's state at the starting point – before
consciously choosing faith or disbelief – must be the same.
However, because light and darkness are relative, the first state
for a believer who acquired brightness during his lifetime is
thought to be dark, and his path towards faith starts from
darkness towards brightness. But the path of the disbeliever starts
from light towards darkness. Thus, the first state for the
disbeliever is light.

Therefore, it is appropriate to examine acquired light and the path
required to obtain it. It is natural, in a comparative manner, to
also turn our focus to acquired darkness, which is attained
through disbelief and sin.

Acquired light

The most important factor that causes the acquisition of light is faith.   Indeed, by attaining faith, humans are exposed to the radiance of Allah (swt).   The Qur'an states:

أَ فَمَن شَرَحَ اللَّهُ صَدْرَهُ لِلاسْلام فَهُوَ عَلَىَ نُورٍ مِّن رَّبِّهِ فَوَيْلٌ لِّلْقَاسِيَةِ
قُلُوبُهُم مِّن ذِكْرِ اللَّهِ أُوْلَئِكَ فِى ضَلال مُّبِين

*Is someone whose breast Allah has opened to Islam so that
he follows a light from His Lord? So woe to those whose
hearts have been hardened to the remembrance of Allah.
They are in manifest error.* (39:22)

This verse demonstrates that we are not in need of producing light. At most, what we must do is open our heart toward the divine light so that it shines over our hearts: "...*the hearts that are in the breasts!*"[1] This is achieved by remembering Allah (swt), a matter which will be discussed later. The Qur'an also states:

أَوَ مَن كَانَ مَيْتًا فَأَحْيَيْنَاهُ وَ جَعَلْنَا لَهُ نُورًا يَمْشِى بِهِ فِى النَّاسِ كَمَن مَّثَلُهُ
فِى الظُّلُمَاتِ لَيْسَ بِخَارِجٍ مِّنْهَا كَذَالِكَ زُيِّنَ لِلْكَفِرِينَ مَا كَانُواْ يَعْمَلُونَ

*Is he who was lifeless, then We gave him life and provided
him with a light by which he walks among the people, like
one who dwells in a manifold darkness which he cannot
leave?* (6:122)

---

[1] Chapter 22 verse 46. The Arabic text is as follows:

«... الْقُلُوبُ الَّتِى فِى الصُّدُور»

If a person lives a faith-based life, a believer who is Allah (swt)-conscious and has strong and true faith in the prophets, he will have light in this world which he will walk with amongst the people: *"O you who have faith! Be wary of Allah and have faith in His Apostle. He will grant you a double share of His mercy and give you a light to walk by."*[1] This light will, in any state – whether in the work environment, in gaining knowledge, or at home – will accompany him to enlighten him and help him make decisions.

Of course, not everyone perceives this light in a believer. Even the believer himself may not sense it directly. What is certain, however, is that its effects can be detected and comprehended. Sometimes the light of faith appears on the face of the believer in a way that will give a kind of attraction and spiritual beauty that will draw the hearts towards him.

When asked as to why those who say night prayer are the best-looking ones, Imam Sajjad replied, "Because they sought solitude with their lord, so Allah (swt) covered them from His light."[2] As said in the Qur'an: *"Their mark is [visible] on their faces, from the effect*

---

[1] Chapter 57 verse 28. The Arabic text is as follows:

«يَـٰٓأَيُّهَا ٱلَّذِينَ ءَامَنُوا۟ ٱتَّقُوا۟ ٱللَّهَ وَ ءَامِنُوا۟ بِرَسُولِهِ يُؤْتِكُمْ كِفْلَيْنِ مِن رَّحْمَتِهِ وَ يَجْعَل لَكُمْ نُورًا تَمْشُونَ بِهِ وَ يَغْفِرْ لَكُمْ وَ ٱللَّهُ غَفُورٌ رَّحِيمٌ»

[2] *Bihar al-Anwar*, vol. 84, p. 159.

of prostration"[1] and "*...The All-Beneficent will endear them [to His creation]*".[2]

On the Day of Judgment this light will be so evident that even the hypocrites will witness it and wish to attain it from the believers. In two verses from chapters *al-Tahrim* and *al-Hadid*, Allah (swt) says that this speedy light will move in front of and from the right side of the believer: "*...With their light moving swiftly before them and on their right*"[3] Perhaps it will move speedily forward so that it guides them towards heaven where they will join the nobles; it will move from the right because they are the People of the Right (*Ashab al-Yamin*) and the book of deeds will be put in their right hand. When the hypocrites see this they will say to the believers, "*Please let up on us, that we may glean something from your light!*,"[4] unaware of the fact that light cannot be borrowed, loaned, or stolen. Each person must have attained this light for himself in the previous life. It is here, among the believers and hypocrites, where a wall with a door will be hoisted. With the rising of this wall the hypocrites can no longer see the believers and their light, though it will be possible to communicate with them.

---

[1] Chapter 48 verse 29. The Arabic text is as follows:

«سِيمَاهُمْ فِي وُجُوهِهِم مِّنْ أَثَرِ السُّجُودِ»

[2] Chapter 19 verse 96. The Arabic text is as follows:

«سَيَجْعَلُ لَهُمُ الرَّحْمَانُ وُدًّا»

[3] Chapter 57 verse 12. The Arabic text is as follows:

«يَسْعَى نُورُهُم بَيْنَ أَيْدِيهِمْ وَ بِأَيْمَانِهِم»

[4] Ibid. verse 13. The Arabic text is as follows:

«انْظُرُونَا نَقْتَبِسْ مِن نُورِكُم»

Presumably, those who have the grounds to obtain forgiveness will head in the direction of this same door. Because this door protects the believers and their light, within the wall dwell the believers and outside the wall dwell the hypocrites; within the wall is the source of protection and mercy and outside the wall is the source of distance and deprivation - a dangerous punishment. The Qur'an says:

يَوْمَ يَقُولُ الْمُنَافِقُونَ وَ الْمُنَافِقَاتُ لِلَّذِينَ ءَامَنُواْ انظُرُونَا نَقْتَبِسْ مِن نُّورِكُمْ قِيلَ ارْجِعُواْ وَرَاءَكُمْ فَالْتَمِسُواْ نُورًا فَضُرِبَ بَيْنَهُم بِسُورٍ لَّهُ بَابٌ بَاطِنُهُ فِيهِ الرَّحْمَةُ وَ ظَاهِرُهُ مِن قِبَلِهِ الْعَذَابُ يُنَادُونَهُمْ أَ لَمْ نَكُن مَّعَكُمْ قَالُواْ بَلَىَ وَ لَكِنَّكُمْ فَتَنتُمْ أَنفُسَكُمْ وَ تَرَبَّصْتُمْ وَ ارْتَبْتُمْ وَ غَرَّتْكُمُ الْأَمَانِى حَتىَ جَاءَ أَمْرُ اللَّهِ وَ غَرَّكُم بِاللَّهِ الْغَرُورُ

The day the hypocrites, men and women, will say to the faithful, 'Please let up on us, that we may glean something from your light!' They will be told: 'Go back and grope for light!' Then there will be set up between them a wall with a gate, with mercy on its interior and punishment toward its exterior. They will call out to them, 'Did we not use to be with you?' They will say, 'Yes! But you cast yourselves into temptation, and you awaited and were doubtful, and [false] hopes deceived you until the edict of Allah arrived, and the Deceiver deceived you concerning Allah. (57:13 & 14)

After faith, the other important source of acquired light is doing righteous deeds. The Qur'an says:

وَ الَّذِينَ ءَامَنُواْ بِاللَّهِ وَ رُسُلِهِ أُوْلَئِكَ هُمُ الصِّدِّيقُونَ وَ الشهُّدَاءُ عِندَ رَبِّهِمْ

لَهُمْ أَجْرُهُمْ وَ نُورُهُمْ وَ الَّذِينَ كَفَرُواْ وَ كَذَّبُواْ بِآيَاتِنَا أُوْلَئِكَ أَصْحَابُ

الجَّحِيم

Those who have faith in Allah (swt) and His apostles — it is they who are the truthful and the witnesses with their Lord; they shall have their reward and their light. But as for those who are faithless and deny Our signs, they shall be the inmates of hell. (57:19)

According to this verse, true faith in Allah (swt) and His prophets – which is the surrendering of the heart coupled with required practice – will raise humans to the rank of the truthful and the witnesses who are the favorites of Allah (swt). Such faith is worthy of divine reward and is also accompanied by light. The deniers of Allah (swt) and His prophets, however, will be deprived and disgraced on the Day of Resurrection. This verse depicts the stages of perfection of the faithful, based on faith itself. It is not that one must pass faith to reach the next stage; rather, the process is in faith itself. The levels of perfection are the same as the levels of faith, and anything other than faith, such as good deeds, are necessitated by faith and can be defined as the dependencies of faith. Perhaps this is why Allah (swt) says in the Qur'an:

إِنَّ الَّذِينَ ءَامَنُواْ وَ عَمِلُواْ الصَّالِحَاتِ يَهْدِيهِمْ رَبُّهُم بِإِيمَانِهِمْ تَجْرِى مِن

تَحْتِهِمُ الأَنْهَارُ فِى جَنَّاتِ النَّعِيم

Indeed those who have faith and do righteous deeds, their Lord guides them by the means of their faith. Streams will run for them in gardens of bliss. (10:9)

In addition to reward, light is also given to the believer (*mumin*). The reward can be in heaven and come in different forms of heavenly blessings. Light, on the other hand, according to the above mentioned verses, is given in this world. It is not that a believer lacks the light of faith and only on the Day of Judgment, after the examination of deeds and determination of rewards is light given to him. Every good deed increases the light of a believer. The following demonstrates examples of some good deeds that give light:

Wudu'

Imam Sadiq is reported to have said regarding *wudu'* (ablution):

أَنَّ الْوُضُوءَ عَلَى الْوُضُوءِ نُورٌ عَلَى نُورٍ وَ مَنْ جَدَّدَ وُضُوءَهُ مِنْ غَيْرِ
حَدَثٍ آخَرَ جَدَّدَ اللَّهُ عَزَّ وَ جَلَّ تَوْبَتَهُ مِنْ غَيْرِ اسْتِغْفَارٍ.

Wudu' upon wudu' is light upon light, and whoever renews his wudu' without [having lost it through] ritual impurity, Allah (swt) will renew his repentance without istighfar [asking forgiveness].[1]

Wudu' is not only a prelude to worship: it is by itself a kind of worship and causes light. Thus, wudu' is not only performed for prayer or other acts of worship that require it; rather, wudu' itself is spiritually significant and one is recommended to be in a constant state of wudu'. What is interesting is that wudu' is a kind of remembrance of Allah (swt) and is a source of proximity;

---

[1] *Man lā Yahduruh-u al-Faqih,* vol. 1, p. 41.

repeating it is beneficial as opposed to physical cleanliness in which washing repeatedly may have no use.

Allah (swt) not only legislated wudu' as a prelude for prayer and as a recommended act in itself; it also has a deep, spiritual effect in the real world (*'alam al-takwin*). The water used for other than wudu' purifies only the external; but when used with the intention of performing wudu', it also attains the power of spiritual purification, and its drops are actually droplets of spiritual purity – or in other words, droplets of light. This is why the water of wudu' must be used in wiping while performing it, and it is recommended (*mustahab*) not to dry the limbs of ablution so that those drops stay on the body for the longest possible time. In early Islam, the Muslims who were aware of its importance used to take the remaining water from the Prophet's wudu' for blessings (*tabarruk*) and would not let a drop of it fall to the ground. As recounted in hadiths, on the Day of Resurrection, the believers' faces are luminous and vibrant as a result of performing wudu' in this world. The Messenger of Allah (swt) said:

يَحْشُرُ اللَّهُ عَزَّ وَ جَلَّ أُمَّتِى يَوْمَ الْقِيَامَةِ بَيْنَ الأُمَمِ غُرّاً مُحَجَّلِينَ مِنْ آثَارِ الْوُضُوءِ.

On the Day of Resurrection, Allah (swt) Almighty will gather my Ummah from among the other nations with white foreheads from the effects of ablution.[1]

If this is the light of ablution, then light of prayer can certainly be described as more luminous.

---

[1] *Bihār al-Anwār*, vol. 77, p. 237.

Hajj

Performing hajj (pilgrimage to Mecca) brings its own light. Concerning the light of Hajj, Imam Sadiq said: "The light of the Hajj ritual remains with a pilgrim so long as he or she does not sin after performing it."[1] Therefore, it is recommended to immediately visit pilgrims upon his return before he sins, resulting in losing his luminance. The Messenger of Allah (swt) said:

> *Then I saw in my dream a man of my Ummah in such a condition that he had darkness in front of him, darkness on his right, darkness on his left, darkness above him, darkness under him—so much so that he was bewildered and baffled, confused, and confounded. Then along came his Hajj and Umrah and both of them took him out of the darkness and both of them placed him in the light.*[2]

Or in the case of a person who shaves, it is recommended to read the following supplication:

----

[1] Ibid. vol. 96, p. 10 & 386. The original text is as follows:

لاَيَزَالُ عَلَى الْحَاجِّ نُورُ الْحَجِّ مَا لَمْ يُذْنِبْ.

[2] Ibid., vol. 7, p. 290. The original text is as follows:

عَنْ عَبْدِ الرَّحْمَنِ بنِ سَمُرَةَ قَالَ كُنَّا عِنْدَ رَسُولِ اللَّهِ (ص) يَوْماً فَقَالَ: [إِنِّى] رَأَيْتُ الْبَارِحَةَ عَجَائِبَ [قَالَ] فَقُلْنَا يَا رَسُولَ اللَّهِ (ص) وَ مَا رَأَيْتَ حَدِّثْنَا [بِهِ] فِدَاكَ أَنْفُسُنَا وَ أَهْلُونَا وَ أَوْلادُنَا إِلَى أَنْ قَالَ قَالَ (ص): رَأَيْتُ رَجُلا مِنْ أُمَّتِي مِنْ بَيْنِ يَدَيْهِ ظُلْمَةً وَ مِنْ خَلْفِهِ ظُلْمَةٌ وَ عَنْ يَمِينِهِ ظُلْمَةٌ وَ عَنْ شِمَالِهِ ظُلْمَةٌ وَ مِنْ تَحْتِهِ ظُلْمَةٌ مُسْتَنْقِعاً فِى الظُّلْمَةِ فَجَاءَهُ حَجُّهُ وَ عُمْرَتُهُ فَأَخْرَجَاهُ مِنَ الظُّلْمَةِ وَ أَدْخَلاهُ فِى النُّورِ

Oh Allah (swt), give me light on the Day of Judgment for
every hair that is shaved.[1]

Looking after Orphans

In his will to Imam Ali, the Prophet (s) said:

يَا عَلِيُّ مَنْ مَسَحَ يَدَهُ عَلَى رَأْسِ يَتِيمٍ تَرَحُّماً أَعْطَاهُ اللَّهُ عَزَّ وَ جَلَّ بِكُلِّ شَعْرَةٍ نُوراً يَوْمَ الْقِيَامَةِ.

O Ali, for those who pass their hands on an orphan's head
as a sign of mercy, Allah (swt) will give them illumination
for every single hair (of that head) on the Day of
Resurrection.[2]

Faith and good deeds

In addition to faith and performing righteous deeds, any kind of
remembrance of Allah (swt) generates light. The Qur'an says:

يَا أَيُّهَا الَّذِينَ ءَامَنُواْ اذْكُرُواْ اللَّهَ ذِكْراً كَثِيراً وَ سَبِّحُوهُ بُكْرَةً وَ أَصِيلاً هُوَ الَّذِى يُصَلِّى عَلَيْكُمْ وَ مَلاَئِكَتُهُ لِيُخْرِجَكُم مِّنَ الظُّلُمَتِ إِلَى النُّورِ وَ كَانَ بِالْمُؤْمِنِينَ رَحِيمًا

O you who have faith! Remember Allah with frequent
remembrance, and glorify Him morning and evening. It is
He who blesses you, and so do His angels, that He may

---

[1] Ibid. vol. 96, p. 304 . The original text is as follows:

قُلِ اللَّهُمَّ أَعْطِنِى بِكُلِّ شَعْرَةٍ نُوراً يَوْمَ الْقِيَامَةِ.

[2] Ibid. vol. 74, p. 60.

bring you out from darkness into light, and He is most merciful to the faithful. (33:41-43)

Commenting on the above verse, the late Allamah Tabataba'i holds that Allah (swt), after his command for abundant remembrance or remembrance as much as possible, states the fact that if you remember Allah (swt) in such a way, Allah (swt) and His Angels will also send their blessings upon you until it drives you from darkness to light. It becomes clear, therefore, that one of the favours and mercies of Allah (swt) in the right of a believer is sending blessings upon him which is the *cause of* leaving darkness and moving toward light. Receiving these blessings is possible with frequent invocation. Therefore, with invocation, one can move toward the source of light and increase his/her light.

In Dua Kumayl we read: *"O Allah (swt), verily I seek nearness to You through remembrance of You."*[1] Also: *"O He whose Name is a remedy and whose remembrance is a cure."*[2] Essentially every being, according to the holy essence of Allah (swt) or His names, is luminous: *"And by the light of Your face, through which all things are illumined!"*[3] In Dua

---

[1] *Iqbal al-a'mal*, vol. 2, p. 707. The original text is as follows:

اللهم انى اتقرب اليك بذكرک.

[2] Ibid. p. 709. The original text is as follows:

يا من اسمه دواء و ذكره شفاء.

[3] Ibid. p. 707. The original text is as follows:

و بنور وجهک الذى أضاء له كل شىء.

'Ahd, we read: *"I beseech Thee in Your Name which lights up the heavens and the earths."* [1]

Once they think of Allah (swt), humans also attain light and tranquility: *"Look! The hearts find rest in Allah (swt)'s remembrance!"* [2] And whenever they turn away from Allah (swt), they will descend into darkness and will have a difficult and dark life: *"But whoever disregards My remembrance, his shall be a wretched life".* [3]

Meanwhile, it becomes clear from here that since the Prophet (s) constantly remembered Him, Allah (swt) and the Angels continually sent salutations to the Prophet (s) and therefore the Prophet (s) always shined as *"a radiant lamp"* [4] and those who follow him are led towards light:

رَّسُولًا يَتْلُواْ عَلَيْكُمْ ءَايَاتِ اللَّهِ مُبَيِّنَاتٍ لِّيُخْرِجَ الَّذِينَ ءَامَنُواْ وَ عَمِلُواْ الصَّالِحَاتِ مِنَ الظُّلُمَاتِ إِلَى النُّورِ

An apostle reciting to you the manifest signs of Allah that He may bring out those who have faith and do righteous deeds from darkness into light. (65:11)

---

[1] *al-Balad al-Amin wa al-Dir' al-Hasin.* The original text is as follows:

و بإسمک الذی اشرقت به السماوات و الارضون.

[2] Chapter 13 verse 28. The Arabic text is as follows:

الَّذِينَ ءَامَنُواْ وَ تَطْمَئِنُّ قُلُوبُهُم بِذِكْرِ اللَّهِ أَلَا بِذِكْرِ اللَّهِ تَطْمَئِنُّ الْقُلُوبُ.

[3] Chapter 20 verse 124. The Arabic text is as follows:

وَ مَنْ أَعْرَضَ عَن ذِكْرِى فَإِنَّ لَهُ مَعِيشَةً ضَنكاً.

[4] Chapter 33 verse 46. The Arabic text is as follows:

سِراجاً مُنِيراً.

In verses 35 through 37 of chapter *al-Noor*, Allah (swt) introduces the places where Allah's light can be reached. After stating that Divine Light is like a niche wherein is a lamp that emits light, He says:

فی بُیُوتٍ أَذِنَ اللَّهُ أَن تُرْفَعَ وَ یُذْکَرَ فِیهَا اسْمُهُ یُسَبِّحُ لَهُ فِیهَا بِالْغُدُوِّ وَ الْآصَالِ رِجَالٌ لَّاتُلْهِیهِمْ تِجَارَةٌ وَلَابَیْعٌ عَن ذِکْرِ اللَّهِ وَ إِقَامِ الصَّلَوةِ وَ إِیتَاءِ الزَّکُوةِ یخَافُونَ یَوْمًا تَتَقَلَّبُ فِیهِ الْقُلُوبُ وَ الْأَبْصَارِ

In houses Allah has allowed to be raised and wherein His Name is celebrated, He is glorified therein, morning and evening, by men whom neither trading nor bargaining distracts from the remembrance of Allah, and the maintenance of prayer and the giving of zakāt. They are fearful of a day wherein the heart and the sight will be transformed. (24:36, 37)

This lamp can be reached in those houses which are places for the remembrance of Allah (swt). It becomes clear that the characteristics of these houses are their connection to those who always remember Allah (swt), and there is nothing that will make them heedless of remembering Him. This remembrance is not merely the remembrance of the heart; rather, it appears in individual and social behaviours such as prayer and alms-giving (zakat). Thus, people who are constantly reminded of Allah (swt) not only become illuminated, their homes also become a place of manifestation and radiance of the Divine's Light, and whoever wants to obtain light could pay heed to Allah (swt) and benefit from His light, considering these houses and the remembrance of Allah (swt) in them.

As stated in both Sunni and Shi'a sources, these houses are the houses of the prophets. It is stated in the exegesis *Al-Durr Al-Manthur* (*The Scattered Pearl*):

قرأ رسول الله (ص) هذه الآية «فِى بُيُوتٍ أَذِنَ اللَّهُ أَنْ تُرْفَعَ» فقام إليه

رجل فقال: أى بيوت هذه يا رسول الله؟ قال: بيوت الأنبياء. فقام إليه

أبو بكر فقال: يا رسول الله هذا البيت منها لبيت على و فاطمة؟ قال:

نعم من أفاضلها.

After the Prophet (saws) read the verse 'In houses Allah (swt) has allowed to be raised' (24:36-37), a man stood up and asked, 'O Messenger of Allah, which are these houses?' to which the Prophet replied, 'The houses of the prophets.' At this time Abu Bakr stood up and, while pointing to the house of Ali and Fatimah, asked, "O Messenger of Allah (swt), is this house among them?" The Prophet said, "Yes, indeed it is one of their best." [1]

Likewise, Ali ibn Ibrahim al-Qummi in his commentary narrates from Jabir from Imam Baqir (as): "They are the houses of the prophets and Ali's house is one of them."[2]

---

[1] *Al-Durr al-Manthur,* vol. 5, p. 50.

[2] *Al-Tafsir al-Qummi,* vol. 2, p. 104. The original text is as follows:

Thus, it is the remembrance of Allah (swt) that causes the light of a person that illuminates the place belonging to him or her. It can be argued that faith also pertains to remembrance. This is why Allah (swt) considers those who lack the light of faith and Islam as hardhearted who are unable to remember Allah (swt):

أَفَمَن شَرَحَ اللَّهُ صَدْرَهُ لِلإسلامِ فَهُوَ عَلَىَ نُورٍ مِّن رَّبِّهِ فَوَيْلٌ لِّلْقَاسِيَةِ قُلُوبُهُم مِّن ذِكْرِ اللَّهِ أُوْلَئِكَ فِي ضَلالٍ مُّبِينٍ

Is someone whose breast Allah has opened to Islam so that he follows a light from His Lord [ad the hardhearted alike]? So woe to those whose hearts have been hardened to the remembrance of Allah. They are in manifest error. (39:22)

عن جابر عن أبى جعفر (ع) فى قوله فى بُيُوتٍ أَذِنَ اللَّهُ أَنْ تُرْفَعَ وَ يُذْكَرَ فِيهَا اسْمُهُ قال: هى بيوت الأنبياء و بيت على (ع) منه.

Bibliography

al-Harrāni, Hasan b. Ali b. Husayn b. Shuʻbah, (1404 A. H.) *Tuhaf al-ʻUqul*, (Qum: Jameah Modarresin)

al-Shirazi, Sadr al-Din Muhammad, (1190), *al-Hikmat al-Muteʻalyia fi al-Asfār al-Arbaʻah*, (Beirut: Dar Ihya' al- Turath al- ʻArabi)

Attributed to Imam Sadiq (a), (1400 A. H.), *Misbah al-Shariʻah*, (Beirut: Aʻlami)

Daylami, Hasan b. Muhammad, (1412 A. H.), *Irshad al-Qolub*, (Qum: al-Sharif al-Radhi)

Guénon, René, (Winter 1973), *Al-Faqr or Spiritual Poverty* in Studies in Comparative Religion

Hurr ʻAmili, Muhammad b. Hasan, (1982), *Al-Jawāhir al-Saniyyah fi al-Ahādith al-Qudsiyyah*, (Beirut: al-Aʻlami li'l-Matbuʻat)

Ibn Babewayh, Muhammad b. Ali, (1413 A. H.), *Man lā Yahduruh-u al-Faqih,* (Qum, Intisharat Islami)

Ibn Fahad Hilli, Ahamad b. Muhammad, (1407 A. H.), *'Uddat al-Da'I*, (Tehran: Dar al-Kutub al-Islamiyah)

Ibn Manzur, Muhammad b. Mokarram, (1414 A. H.), *Lisan al-'Arab*, (Beirut: Dār al- Fikr)

Ibn Tawus, Ali b. Musa, (1409 A. H.), *Iqbal al-a'mal*, (Tehran: Dar al-Kutub al-Islamiyah)

Imām Ali (a), *Nahj al-Balaghah (Sobhi Salih)*, compiled by Muhammad b. Husayn, Sharif al-Radhi, (Qum: Hijrat, (1414 A.H.)

Imam Zain al-Abidin (a), (1987), *The Psalms of Islam*, tr. Chittick, Willliam C., (Qum: Ansariyan Pbulications)

Kulayni Muhammad, (1407 A. H.), *Usul al-Kafi*, (Tehran: Dar al-Kutub al-Islamiyah)

Majlesi, Muhammd Baqir, (1403 A.H.), *Bihār al-Anwār*, (Beirut: Dar Ihya' al- Turath al- 'Arabi)

Ms'udi, Ali b. Husayn, (1426 A. H.), *Ithbat al-Wasilah*, (Qum: Ansariyan)

Nurbakhsh, Javad, *Spiritual Poverty in Sufism*, tr. Leonard Lewisohn

Nuri, Husayn b. Muhammad Taqi, (1408), *Mustadrak Wasā'il*, (Qum: Alu'l-Bayt (a))

Payandeh, Abu al-Qasim, Nahj al-Fasāha, (Tehran: Donyaeh Danesh)

Rumi, *Mathnawi*

Tabātabā'i, Sayyid Muhammad Husayn, (1974), *al-Mizan fi Tafsir al-Qur'an*, (Beirut: al-A'lami li'l-Matbu'at)

Tamimi, Abd al-Vahid b. Muhammad, (1410 A. H.), *Ghurar al-Hikam wa Durra al-Kalim*, (Qum: Dar al-Kutub al-Islami)

Kaf'ami, Ibrahim b. Ali 'ameli, (1418 A. H.), *al-Balad al-Amin wa al-Dir' al-Hasin*, (Beirut: al-A'lami li'l-Matbu'at)